Parthian Words

A Carcanet BOOK

NOVELS

That was Yesterday
A Day Off
Europe to Let
Cousin Honoré
Cloudless May
Before the Crossing *and* The Black Laurel
The Green Man
The Hidden River
Road from the Monument
The Blind Heart
The Early Life of Stephen Hind
The White Crow

NON-FICTION

Modern Drama in Europe
No Time Like the Present
The Writer's Situation
The Journal of Mary Hervey Russell
Journey from the North—*Autobiography*

Storm Jameson

Parthian Words

Harper & Row, Publishers
New York, Evanston, San Francisco, London

1817

FIRST U.S. EDITION

STANDARD BOOK NUMBER: 06-012176-9

LIBRARY OF CONGRESS CATALOG CARD NUMBER: 70-123937

Contents

Foreword

Few moments in a life are more disconcerting than the one in which a long carefully guarded plan is seen to have powdered – as we say of old wood. My intention, when I was at an age to intend confidently, was to become a critic, possibly a don, and bring up to date a work I read and re-read from the day I discovered it in the library of my university: George Saintsbury's *History of Criticism*. It is not necessary to say that I was completely unqualified to judge it, I was simply an undergraduate with a craze.

The first book I wrote, a study of modern drama in Europe, based on my M.A. thesis, earned me several columns of wholehearted abuse from the well-found elderly critics of the subject: these included A. B. Walkley and St John Ervine: I was too far ahead of the time when impudence became a merit. This sharp check to my ambitions, and a habit I had fallen into of mismanaging my life, tricked me into a career as a professional novelist and into what, speaking of himself, Julien Benda called 'une assez grande situation d'homme obscur', and relegated to the far back of my mind the critical works I projected. It is many years too late to blow the dust off them: I have barely time to arrange in some kind of order – less an order than a succession of dissolving views – the dispassionate comments of an old fiction hand, a strictly personal exercise of taste and judgement, barely a footnote to the work of my great mentor. Since writing is inextricably entangled with the other threads of my life – I was for so long little more than a *machine à écrire* – my opinions on writing and the other arts are inextricably part of my views on society. In a sense this short book is the moral autobiography of a writer as well as an essay in criticism. All things considered – and to borrow again from Benda, writing in solitude in Carcassonne during the years between 1940 and 1944 – it should be called *Exercise d'un enterré vif*.

I am sure of offending a great many solemn persons. I should admit at once that I have been marked for life by my long respectful friendship with Stendhal and the great Russians. This has meant and means that again and again as I pick my way, with and without pleasure, through the lively brilliant crowd of contemporary novelists, the shadow of these great ghosts falls across the sunlit or incense-laden scene and the whole land-scape pales and dwindles. This is a disadvantage I shall never be able to remove.

Further, I cannot pretend to be competent to judge any but English fiction, and I am widely read only in English, French and American. My knowledge of the fiction of other countries, since I can only read it in translation into English or French has inexcusable gaps. None the less, the field I have botanised in is a very rich one, the richer for its border of wind-blown seeds, a Pasternak, a Jorge Luis Borges, a Solzhenitsyn, a Machado do Assis, a Silone, a Musil, a Günter Grass – the proportions are very chancy, probably four Germans or Russians to one Portuguese or one Italian.

I have, too, in my favour an intense curiosity about the intellectual habits of writers of fiction. My own errors have taught me to read certain signs. I know why X. has never written the novels his friends expected of him when he was younger: deflected from them not only by a preference for his own library and the south of France, but by the critic always at his elbow. The difference between him and me, and between me and Y. and Z., busy contented novelists, is that I know and they do not (or do not admit to themselves) that for all our

8

talent, hard work, attempts at honesty, our small *aperçus*, tiny flashes of originality and the rest, a few weeks or months after we die not a syllable of our works will break the surface of oblivion. We turn the handles of our barrel-organs in the street, here one minute and dead the next. To think anything else is folly. We write because we must, and because it gives us, on the whole, pleasure.

To write this little book has brought together the two ends of a circle started half a century ago in the energy of first youth and broken at once. Hence I have been able to write as I wrote then – without trying to please, and without its entering my head that I might give offence. Fifty years ago I was afraid of nothing and no one. Now, after an interval of half a century, I am once more – for a good reason – without fear. Hence, too, the months of nearly complete happiness its writing has given me, a little the happiness enjoyed by the writer I love this side idolatry, whose *vrai métier* was, he said, *d'écrire un roman dans un grenier.*

1. How often do you read a new novel twice?

Nothing in the literary world – if it is a world and not rather a fair-ground – is stranger, more paradoxical, than the figure cut today by the novel. Here is an immense industry, kept going by an immense investment in it of intelligence, observation, humour, lively invention – scarcely a year without its bene-diction of at least one novel which impresses by its thoughtful-ness, wit, sincerity, what you will; even, at longer intervals, a novel which can be read again and again, a *Doctor Zhivago*, a *Mort d'un personnage*, an *Il Gattopardo*. It would not be easy to find a country that lacked its two or three living novelists to be respected for a body of work with the virtues of *Darkness at Noon*, *La condition humaine*, *Recollection of a Journey*, *Les célibataires*, *The Bright Day*, *Bread and Wine*, *A Legacy*, *Les horreurs de l'amour* . . . the list could be trebled or quadrupled. It remains that, since the death of Proust, Musil, Joyce, D. H. Lawrence, the contemporary novels which matter a great deal could be got into a single modest bookcase, and one of the most notable of these living writers, André Malraux, ceased in 1943 to write fiction, some six or seven years after the ap-pearance of his most impressive work. (Perhaps just as well he did. Eloquence, although it had not reached the suffocating luxuriance of parts of the first volume of *Antimémoires*, was starting to overgrow his imagination.)

A trace of pity or contempt has crept into comments on the novel, not so often of Grub Street reviewers – apt, an occupa-tional risk, to bless with genial and undiscriminating piety, an automatic laying on of hands – as of lettered critics and readers.

These compare the vast resources of intelligence and industry used to produce a huge output of fiction (still huge, in spite of sinking numbers) with the briefness of the impression made by novels which spring up, are praised, endure for a season, and in a grievously short time are cut down and wither. It would be difficult to quarrel with their verdict. Hand on your heart, do you recall with any certainty who bedded whom in the last but one of Miss Murdoch's verbal ballets, or in any detail the social and sexual activities of persons invented three or four years ago by so admirably serious a writer and moralist as Mr Angus Wilson? In the last year or two you must have read at least one novel, probably by a woman, which as you read it struck you as thoughtful, perceptive, written with care and ambition – and bound for oblivion, one character merging into another, to become a bloodless spectral swarm, then a vapour. Now and then, very rarely, one of these persists: a piercingly fresh voice breaks through (the voice, say, of Piers Paul Read in *Game in Heaven with Tussy Marx*), or some principle of growth or strangeness in a novel which keeps it alive for a time and fecund. In every such instance I know of, it has been written by a writer who would seem to have had the patience to wait for his novel to be born rather than give it premature test-tube birth.

It is not unjust to say of many admirable new novels that they have been written to meet the taste and needs of cultivated even intellectual worldlings. Subtle, graceful, sentient, exciting, amusing, sometimes acute, they demand neither time nor a great deal of attention. The acid test of any novel is: Shall I want to read this again and again, at intervals throughout my life, as I re-read *War and Peace* and the *Chartreuse de Parme*? If the answer is an instant No, then in what way, in what essential way, does the most skilful and knowing work of fiction differ, except in length, from the social occasional verse of a good minor poet?

We are too quick to forget that the enduring novels are those it is impossible *not* to put down, because the mind cannot bear so much deep disturbance and tension without intervals of escape.

There can never have been a time when so many novels to be admired for their technical skill, their invention, mother wit, acumen, were being written. It is mortifying to our vanity that so few, so very few of them can be re-read even once – *ce sont de ces livres qu'on ne lit que d'une main.* Very few do not give up in a single reading all, much or little, they have in them to give. The deep sources, the echoes, are missing. Constant re-reading does not exhaust *A la recherche du temps perdu,* but how many of us dip twice into the endless flow of social trivia, on its level interesting, which pours from the pens or typewriters of contemporary novelists, urbane in a Powell, boisterously vigorous in an Amis, a Burgess, sensible and graceful in a score of thoughtful middle-aged women writers? To think incautiously of Stendhal and the great Russians, or on another level of James or Conrad, is to see the novels of these living writers, concerned with the accurate reproduction of small immediate realities, social, personal, fade to a weak pencil mark. It is almost as though, like so many of the efficient products of a consumers' society, they number among their qualities a built-in obsolescence to make replacement by a newer model easy, by any newer model on offer from a talented swarm of younger women and rather fewer young men. It is at once rash to say bluntly of a contemporary: A year or ten minutes after his death he will be extinct, and impossible to believe that the ashes of any one of us, lively epigones, will blaze when a friend stirs them, like the ashes of Kafka.

What is missing in these seriously and carefully written problems of men and women, in love, in marriage, in professions, in adultery, in rivalry with one another, in misery and bliss, is not, but not, intelligence, insight, observation, fantasy, speculation. Missing is any firm trace of a person behind the millions of words, that sense so clear and vital in the work of the Victorian giants and the half-giants their immediate successors, few of whom had the dexterity of today's novelists, or the verbal audacity. An almost naïve publicity turned on by television, by the gossip columns of the weeklies and the supplements of newspapers, lights up a silhouette, and another and another. But the force, the towering presence, still to be felt behind the signs made by a few nineteenth-century writers, is just not there.

It would be absurd to make an effort to remember singly any green shoot of the crop of semi-fiction written by very young women or young men engrossed in their own fledgling exciting lives, novels forgotten in the instant of turning the last pages. No one tells these poor clever children, no one was kind enough to tell me, that truths of body and soul take half a lifetime to begin to learn, and that my Uncle Toby's comment on the great Lipsius, composer of a work the day he was born, could not be more apt to their case, as it was to mine. Neither does any good soul warn them of the demoralising effect on a half-empty or immature mind of gulping down a great genitor. Even Henry James can scarcely with complete safety be put into stripling hands. Still less, Joyce or Freud: that young man reeling away from his first dram of *Ulysses*, blindly sure that now, now, he knows how novels must be written, is not in a state to know the worth of his own thin stream of consciousness.

Infinitely less forgivable, more impudent, more damaging to the reputation of the novel in our day, the manufacture, with film and paperback rights in view, of completely worthless – what is the right term? these artifacts are not novels, they bear no relation to literature or life, they have no sensuous or other graces. I suppose that without the existence of the new markets, reputable firms would not accept them for publication. A new label should be found to describe what are strictly speaking non-novels.

None of these absurdities is material. What matters, what is to be coolly examined, is the dictum, repeated by so many solemn and respectable persons, that virtue has gone out of the modern novel: cleverness and talent galore, but no living novelist with the divine or devilish energy to create a world one can return to again and again as to a loved city, at each visit finding new aspects, streets not yet walked in, a changed light, inhabitants, recognised from earlier visits, still living their varied lives from day to day. Add, in parenthesis, that it is not always the handsome cities to which one returns most readily: certain corners of a dull little town, a square without pretensions and blessed with a friendly café, a certain calm light falling across a naked hill, can provoke a more intense pleasure than Chartres.

Are they right, these respectable persons? They may be. But give me a little time.

In the meantime I am forgetting one immediately noticeable mark – noticed by foreigners such as the very distinguished Frenchman exiled in London during the last war who told me with the greatest politeness that he would try to learn English if I could assure him that anything was being written which he ought to read – of the novel in this country is its parochialism, endearing if you like, but a little airless, and short-breathed. Could it be that our escape from the ordeal, far worse than air-raids, of invasion, occupation by a foreign army and police, delations, torture, opened a gap between us and other European nations, forcing us back into our parish? Hence the pleasure to be got from Olivia Manning's evocations of Bucharest and Athens, from Paul Scott's sensuous and solid knowledge of India, and Sarah Gainham's of the European cock-pit, and from the work of an older living English writer, half a dozen of whose novels – I doubt he has written more than twice that number – really stretch the minds of readers beyond the boundaries of their familiar world, really widen our vision of the possibilities of human nature, and insist on being attended to as we attend to Conrad: R. C. Hutchinson, whose misfortune – or fortune – is to have entered on his maturity as a novelist at a point in time when to stand, modestly and politely, in the central tradition of English fiction is to invite respectful neglect.

Possibly the sharp taste of Graham Greene's writing is due equally to his wilful exposure of his mind to the Africas and seedy underworlds of our infernal century and to his participation in the intellectual system of the Catholic Church. Like Brecht, another writer whose work we do not quickly forget, he struggled to get his breath inside a powerful orthodoxy and mutely in conflict with it. It gives his fiction a bony structure.

I have just looked up the word parochialism in the Oxford English Dictionary: 'confinement of one's interests to a narrow sphere, with indifference to the world outside; local narrowness of view; petty provincialism.' Before I am reminded that an extraordinary novelist can uncover in a parish the size of a village street the lineaments of heaven and hell, let me say that I know it. By parochialism I mean X's amiable interest in the seduction of a pretty girl by a lightweight Don Juan, or Y's solemn absorption in the emotions of a female don or a dissatisfied wife or any one of the stock figures of domestic life in a Woman's Page world.

2. Has the novel gone into a decline?

Critics have been amusing themselves for a long time by aus-
cultating fiction for signs of heart failure. In 1948 Lionel Trill-
ing wrote: 'It is impossible to talk about the novel without
having in our minds the question of whether it is still a living
force. Twenty-five years ago T. S. Eliot said that the novel
came to an end with Flaubert and James . . . This opinion is now
heard on all sides.' The image is of a gathering of consultants in
the ante-room while the patient fights for breath at the other
side of the door.

About the same time a rather more umbrageous critic, Cyril
Connolly, said: 'Flaubert, Henry James, Joyce, and Virginia
Woolf have finished off the novel.' The verdict now is one of
murder. In the second degree? By inadvertence?

Much earlier, in 1929, with the naïveté of my age I wrote,
'No conscientious novelist but reflects, a hundred times during
the writing of a book into which he is putting all he knows,
that it is after all hardly worth while . . . that what he is making
is not even an approximation to truth . . . The more sensitive
a mind, the more fastidiously it turns from the distorting
medium of fiction . . . Examples might be multiplied, but
none of them has the force and validity of the confused feeling
which assures us that the best work of the best modern novelist
is not in so high a class as, say, *Undertones of War*.'

Forgive me, I was brought up a Parnassian, in the innocent
belief that the novel's place is below the other arts, on the
lowest slope of the hill, its feet sunk in the earth.

Last year an anonymous voice from *The Times Literary*

Supplement, our nearest approach to the divine right (tempered by a disarming mediocrity) of the French Academy, spoke about the survival of the horse as a luxury and went on: 'The situation of the arts in the twentieth century is analogous. They also have been made redundant by technological progress, and the first task of criticism ought to be to discover how this came about and what precisely has replaced them. So far most of those who practise and write about the arts have been reluctant to face this situation frankly, partly because they have the excuse that novels – even thrillers – are not yet actually written by computers, but mainly because no class of person is enthusiastic about writing its own obituary . . .'

With the least trouble in the world I could find a score of like quotations. Like only in that they agree on the chronic invalidism of the modern novel. Unlike in the reasons they offer. Did the novel reach a peak of felicity and refinement with Flaubert, James, Joyce and a few others, from which in the nature of things, only decline is possible, like the inevitable stiffening and weakening of a highly cultivated mind? Are the new powerful media spoiling the novelist's chosen country? Or, as I was simple enough to believe in 1929, is the complexity of the world now so monstrous as to defeat any novelist who attempts a complete picture?

The last notion can be discarded out of hand. No writer, not even Tolstoy, not even Balzac, attempted a complete picture, even of a single life. Why should he? The consummate humanity and visionary reach of the *Oresteia* is not made less by Aeschylus's indifference to the problems of the trading and slave classes in Athens, nor Proust's by his almost exclusive interest in the upper reaches of Parisian society. Slightly closer to us – since in the three parts of *Die Schlafwandler* Hermann Broch could make imaginative sense of thirty years (1888-1918) of foundering social and moral values and their violent collapse into chaos, why need we assume that it would be impossible for a novelist to deal as maturely with the thirty-eight years since 1930?

True, the complexity has become excessive and barbarous. True, it is harder for fiction to integrate and expose the intellectual ferment and modes of being of an age in which every moral assumption of the past is challenged and shaken as a child shakes a handful of weeds, and scientific and mathematical thought is stretching the fabric of existence out of sight and sense of ordinary men and women. The nineteenth-century novelist could still comfortably repeat that all the world's a stage and call together enough of the cast to give a vivid intimation of the whole. We no longer know towards what the theatre is evolving, nor whether the performance is to go on tomorrow night. True, too, that no novelist now living has made the effort to recreate the world of 1969 either through an exploration in depth of an individual consciousness, or in an epic narrative. But need we be sure that that is because the effort really is too great for any one mind? Or is it a refusal – like the refusal of a horse at a fence? Is it evidence that the effort could not, given the ferocious energy of mind, body, spirit, called for, be made? Or only evidence that a novelist with the architectural genius of a Proust or a Tolstoy, able to imagine his immense novel as a whole, is not at hand?

Might it be that like Simeon we wait for a birth?

In the meantime we are not without the occasional *roman fleuve*. Great talent and even greater industry went into the writing of Jules Romains's *Les hommes de bonne volonté*, but it is essentially a series of separate novels, some wholly admirable, some contrived. And this is true of the few in progress in England, even when they have the spinal thread of an omnipresent character. They form terraces of houses, varying in solidity and charm, not a city.

Lacking the architectural vision, a dominant theme serves as mortar – as in Arnold Zweig's superb trilogy of the First

World War, shaped, animated, by his humane curiosity about faulty passionate human beings caught up in the age-old conflict between justice and expediency.

Does anyone now read *The Case of Sergeant Grischa, Education Before Verdun, The Crowning of a King*? Or is not only the supreme novelist of our age missing, but his audience?

*

Can we look more closely at the difficulties in the contemporary novelist's way?

Sooner or later, as they tip-toe towards the sick room, critics begin talking about the effect on him of the electronic revolution. With a certain pudor – very creditable – they avert their eyes from one of the effects: that a novelist – any novelist, well-known, or not known at all, the fledgling author of a single novel – may wake up to find himself richer by a large sum paid him for the film rights of his book. These accidents have no bearing on the life and death of the novel. They change the life of one novelist. That is all. They do not affect, either for good or ill, the writer's situation as an atom in a society increasingly dominated by electronic technology.

A critic inclined to melancholy sees the poor fellow on the way to becoming a half-tolerated member of a small sophisticated élite holding itself aloof from a mass drugged into contentment or sullen boredom by spectator sports and television. Will he find that his imagination cannot breathe in the space left for it? Shut himself in his tower to contemplate the human condition? Try to draw his nourishment, like Cavafy, from some Byzantine past? For whom? For his own amusement? He will need the arrogance of a Joyce and the sublime indifference to an audience of a great prince. He will need, too, a private income: Joyce had to be supported when he was writing his two long novels. There will be no Africas of the spirit for the self-exile of a new Rimbaud, and no primitive society from which new seeds might come.

Exaggeratedly romantic? I think so, but I am willing to agree with the pessimist of the *Literary Supplement* that if the novel, like the horse, is in danger of becoming a survival, the new media of communication – wireless and television, and on a different level the computer – are partly responsible. These sacred monsters cannot replace the novelist, but they can displace him, elbow him out of the market and deflect him from his proper business: to share his life experience with those of his fellows who are willing to attend patiently while he unfolds it with the strictest veracity and frankness of which he is capable. Something he will not be able to do through the public channels of the electronic age.

Marshall McLuhan tediously overdoes his flash of insight. But it is true that we are herded on the frontiers of an age in which the printed book is being overtaken by the new media much as the hand-copied manuscript was overtaken by the invention of print. The shift is only beginning; it will never be total, into however many departments of literature modern technology intrudes. Complacency would be fatuous. Already I, to whom it has never occurred to think that literacy can rest on anything but the habit of private reading, am as absurd an anachronism as a medieval scholar who disliked the look of a printed page and held on to his parchments. A wireless talk means little to me until I have read it, and a television argument bores me by compelling me to attend to it with the ear I use for listening to external noises and an eye not used to continual shifts of focus. It gives me no pleasure to reflect that I am going through an experience in company with millions of my kind: my nervous system rejects a forced involvement, in one vast mechanically begotten community, with the nervous systems of every other listener and watcher. It rebels against the demoralising pressure of information thrust on it from all

sides. Moreover, by refusing to learn the new habit I am wilfully holding aloof, trying obstinately to live by the habits of
a past age, trying to take refuge in an artificial oasis of silence
and privacy, a monastery without walls. It can be done – at a
psychological cost.

No doubt I could train myself to take in by ear more than I
do. That is not the point. Nor is it relevant that three-fifths – I
am being benevolent – of the entertainment offered is crude
and shoddy. To mock the new media is too easy. It is plainly
not because miracles of technology can and often are used to
disseminate brain-softening half-truths and nonsense that they
are the novelist's enemies. Has he not always, since the onset of
semi-literacy, had to keep his head above the flood of *kitsch*?
The strident new media are his enemies because they exist, and
create habits not merely unlike but actively opposed to the
habits of a man sitting down to take part in a dialogue with
the writer of the book in his hand. However admirable a talk,
an argument, a poem, a narrative, read out on the wireless, it
has to be listened to with a sort of attention which allows the
hearer no time to play his part in the dialogue. Worse, mind
and senses become habituated – that is, hardened – by the
incessant flow of sounds and visible images into millions of
eyes and ears, and the instantaneous appearance to them of
events taking place anywhere in a world fast dwindling, in Mr
McLuhan's lively metaphor, to a tribal encampment. It is
possible that a public ritual, on this level, is filling, with something, the void left when the rituals of the church ceased to be
a common experience. With something. With a farce or a state
funeral or the agonised face of a man about to be put to death in
another country.

For the writer, as for more adaptable mortals, the problem is
not how to escape from the machine, but to discover how he
can be free in relation to it. I do not for an instant hope that the
media of mass communication can be used to transmit the

imaginative vision even of an accomplished patently sincere woman novelist, infinitely less that of a Proust, a Kafka, a Pasternak. I believe it to be inevitable that, for a mass audience, emotive language will always have to be thinned down, denuded of the utmost awareness, the utmost subtlety of which a serious writer is capable. The peculiar oddity of words as signs is that they point two ways, backward to the origin of language in the neurological structure of the brain and immediately forward. Language is memory and metaphor, it stores up the experience of the race and translates it into infinitely ancient words. Behind the written word there is the oral tradition, the echoes go back to the child hearing his mother's voice say *bread* or *house*, and beyond it. In any words, even the most primitive, there is an emotional residue untranslatable into other words and never wholly communicable. The most intimate meanings of English elude the inner ear of a man born to use another tongue. It is on this deepest oldest sense of language that poetry and precise subtle prose call. We learned, some few centuries ago, to translate the printed or written word back effortlessly into these buried subtleties of sound and sense, to send them through the eye to the inner remembering ear of a reader who is attending not only to the words but to their endless echoes in his mind. This same reader may, as scientist or scholar, draw on the prodigious memory of an electronic brain. Unless he is insensible he knows that there are memories he cannot draw on except in the millennial communion of one man speaking to another, without haste, in solitude. The gap between what the writer means and what he is able to say can be closed only in the silence during which the attentive eye transmits and the attentive brain hears the words on the page.

A curious feeling, a little that of a savage or an animal at the onset of an eclipse, seizes me when I am shown an advanced type of computer. Not long ago a highly respected writer grumbled to me, 'We may, in a hundred or more years, be able to civilise television, if enough of us survive and if we can get a foot in past the Susan Nippers in possession. We shall never defeat the computer, the brute thinks.'

In one sense he was not talking nonsense. A writer whose life has been spent cultivating the finer shades of his language cannot help feeling misplaced in a world he shares with machines which extend the human brain as massively as television and wireless extend our eyes, ears, and nervous system. There is something obscurely menacing about a machine advanced enough to devise its own problems and learn from its mistakes. Irrationally, the writer is irritated and embarrassed by it. His sense of being in some indefinable way threatened does not spring from anything the brute does which directly affects him. When an electronic expert tells me that in the foreseeable future computers will be doing the work of painters and poets, I know that his notion of what goes on in the mind of painter and poet is laughably crude. The slow, infinitely complex process of *improvisation* at depth which is literature can be mimed by a machine, but not conceived, not given breath and motion. There are two kinds of communication possible through words and images. There is the communication of information, and this the computer can be made to deliver with incomparable speed and efficiency. And there is the communication of a profound insight into the kernel of the human spirit. I know in my writer's bones and in the marrow of my bones that this will never be provided by the most fantastically intricate and advanced machine.

None the less, when I think of the yet unrealised potentialities of the computer I feel discomfort and a confused sense of being in some way diminished. This has nothing to do with puerilities about computer poetry and drama. It has deeper roots – in an impotent only half explicit resentment of the god in the machine, a man-made god endowed by human ingenuity with inhuman powers.

I have no furtive sense that the electronic-magnetic discoveries revolutionising our world are intrinsically anti-
human. As our mothers told us, there is a place for everything
when everything is in its place. A place for that extension of our
senses and brain which is the computer and Early Bird, and a
place for the one-to-one communion in which we come face
to face with ourselves in a book. Neither our dead nor our unborn can reach us in any other way, by any but this channel of
living water.

*

'The role of the poet in our society and in the life of words has
greatly diminished. Most of the sciences are wholly out of his
grasp and he can impose on only a narrow range of the
humanities his ideals of clear and inventive discourse.' (George
Steiner.)

I could not find other words as direct as these, written in
1961, to convey the modern novelist's sense, conscious and
unconscious, that in the past half-century his charter to order
and criticise life had been woefully eroded. What can a novelist
who is at best a contemporary of Newton – and it may be only
of Galileo – make of the mental universe of the Nobel
scientist? The amazement he feels when confronted by a physicist's achievement, not one syllable of which he understands
– supposing, which is entirely unlikely, that it is expressed in
syllables and not in mathematical signs – is only too excusable.
None the less, and *pace* the eminent critic, I find needless and
disconcerting the diffidence of an imaginative writer in face
of the closed universe – closed not only to him – of scientific
thought.

It is not only the physicist who can overawe the novelist. I
can understand his being fascinated by psychoanalysis, Marx-
ism, existentialism, sociology, linguistics, anthropology, disciplines which, except the last two in their metaphysical reaches,

use language in ways he is familiar with. But why should he let their practitioners interfere with his own discipline, fundamentally opposed in conception and aim to the discipline of science? His is a radically different use of language, to convey an attitude to life, as distinct from dissecting, analysing, classifying its forms and origins. When I was younger, I approached politely novels in which terms detached from their rightful context litter the pages as tiresomely as sacred cows drift about a Delhi street: complex, fixation, the *néant*, alienation, and the rest and the rest, jargon. Now, without disrespect, I prefer to use my leisure in less arid ways. Oedipus is a more moving and ironically significant figure as imagined by Sophocles (or even Cocteau) than as the maladjusted case dissected in one of last week's novels: Racine and Proust expose jealousy with a nakedness infinitely more shocking than the academically distanced images of Robbe-Grillet in *Jalousie*. It is curious what a sterilising effect a knowledge of psychoanalytic technique has on the novelist who uses it overtly, even when he understands what he is saying. Not long ago I read a first novel by an intelligent man who chose to serve up his knowledge raw, not fired by his imagination but laid out in alternate chapters of narrative and informed discussion of Freudian doctrine and methods. With the result that the characters spent more than half their time in a state of suspended animation, and what might have been a novel became a jerky series of fictional footnotes to a treatise on psycho-pathology. It served the author right. He should not have asked Freud to write his novel for him instead of making the effort to transmute a theory into terms proper to literature.

When a writer with pretensions to intellectual audacity writes: 'I think there's going to be more and more merging of art and science. Scientists are already studying the creative process, and I think the whole line between art and science will break down and that scientists, I hope, will become more creative and writers more scientific,' it is either naïveté or illiteracy – if it is not a hardworking publicist's wish to share in the respect paid to scientists in the nuclear age.

Mr William Burroughs need not be taken seriously. But not many weeks ago I was saddened to see an elderly writer I admire listening, with something near hangdog meekness, to the strictures on his latest novel made by a scientific don. 'Not,' the young man said courteously, 'that your work is unintelligent, it is merely irrelevant to the *real problems*; these can only be tackled along empirical or statistical lines. Your struggles to find what you call meaning in life is nothing better than a shocking waste of a good mind.'

He moved away, and I approached the elderly novelist – and reproached him.

'No one,' I said, 'can know everything. The Goethean ideal of an educated man is meaningless. No one can understand with an equal profundity Homer, Dante, Shakespeare and the Double Helix. Why should you imagine that your wisdom is in some way inferior to that of a physicist, even one more famous than your young friend?'

'Because,' he answered, with some violence, 'it is idiotic to deny that today science is *the* instrument of understanding. The tremendous steps it is making, the conquest of space, the even more remarkable conquest of the nuclear space – I don't even know how to phrase that – the shattering changes it is making in our lives – in a few short years a greater change than that from ape to man . . . You have no answer to that.'

Dialectic is not my forte. It was several hours before I came on an answer. I offer it with conviction, modestly. The value of a thinker's achievement, physicist or novelist, is not to be measured by the startling nature of the changes it makes in human lives. A drab subordinate fellow called Eichmann and his equally unimaginative associates changed the lives of several millions of men, women and children in the space of five years.

So did the prisoners in the dock at Nuremburg, who stood there, as a spectator noted in his diary, looking 'drab, depressing, ill . . . It seems incredible that such a dim set of men should or could have done such huge and dreadful things.'

The scientist is changing our lives in unnumbered huge ways, many of them humane, a few of them dreadful. He is not able to change us emotionally and morally as a few works of imagination have changed us, and still, as each generation comes to them again, do. The *real problems* of man in this day and age still relate to the quality of our daily bread, material and spiritual, still turn on the difficulty of living as a whole man in a morally and intellectually fragmented world. I would sooner seek the advice on this of one of the great novelists, of Tolstoy or Stendhal or Emily Brontë, than of the greatest of physicists. Unless he is an impostor, the novelist's researches into the springs of human nature make demands on his intellect and intuition no less exacting than those made on the scientist investigating an aspect of the physical world we are all embedded in. To be, in his field, the equal of the scientist he has not only to probe the deeper levels of his own and his fellow-creatures' motives, but find a language purged of sentimentality – *Je tremble toujours*, said Stendhal, *de n'avoir écrit qu'un soupir quand je crois avoir noté une vérité* – in which to present his sensuous and intellectual discoveries to the minds and senses of his readers. The effort of a lifetime is not long enough to seize in all its complexity, its infinite possibilities, the experience he wants to translate into words. Nor is the reality he can expose of less passionate interest or less vitally necessary to us than that exposed by the scientist. It is vital, precise, passionate, in a different sense.

The flaw in this argument is that – to change our lives – the novelist must be listened to. Exercising his right 'to slake his earnest and zealous thirst after knowledge and understanding', the physicist can not only change our lives but may bring them to a sudden stop, whether we were attending to him or not. In the public eye, this gives him an overwhelming importance, a little the importance primitive man gave his priest-shaman.

To admit it does not justify the writer in thinking himself less required and able than his fellow the scientist to try, in all humility, to impose on the chaos of the world 'his ideals of clear and inventive discourse.'

*

In his grittily sensible way the Marxist critic knows precisely when and why the novel began its decline into modishness.

It is not because they are abnormally greedy for notice, or forced (now that even a garret costs) to make money quickly, or are ashamed to be less successful than a tenth-rate pop singer (as most of them are), or find (as most of them do) the novels of their fathers' generation tediously irrelevant to the ideals and desires of an era of total sexual freedom, nor is it because Flaubert and James have exhausted the soil, that novelists of a later breed would as soon make a habit of family prayers as look in themselves for the patience and religious self-assurance of a George Eliot – or, come to that, a Conrad. The author of *Middlemarch* and her immediate successors were the intellectual shadow thrown by a solidly-established bourgeois world with a common economic and social language and a fairly common habit of paying its respects to the virtues of tolerance (within safe limits), the value and rights of the individual as defined by his status, and the power of reason, if not to get rid of violently inconvenient emotions, at least to name their causes and find ways to control them. Not that the great nineteenth-century novelists were unaware of problems and the tragic predicaments forced on the individual when his passions came into conflict with the social norms, but since they did not repudiate these norms in themselves they were able to go on writing from a secure centre. George Eliot might be torn with pity for unhappy frustrated men and women, but she was not torn in herself: hence, whatever form she threw her novel into, using a familiar tool, she was unequivocally at home in it, corsetted only by the duty to respect certain proprieties which in sober fact she was very willing to respect.

At his ease inside this seemingly unshakable structure, the classic novelist had good grounds for believing that he could examine rationally the motives of a character created in his image – even when he was concerning himself with the errors of a man unable to adjust himself to the laws of class and property and the ethos erected on them. He could even condemn abuses marring a society he had no impulse to overthrow, saw no reason to overthrow.

Its decline involved his. With the disregarded dignity of a once wealthy, now impoverished old lady, the novel bred from his certainties has little acceptable to say to an age of economic breakdown, violent political earthquakes, the triumph of doctrines contemptuous of individual freedom, the growing revelation of irrational depths in human nature itself, the withering away of every obstacle to sexual enjoyment inside and outside marriage and all the radical social and psychological changes this implies. What questions the age asks, it does not ask of the old lady. The sense of change and breakdown is reflected in contemporary fiction at two extremes. At one extreme in its most revolutionary, most aggressively experimental forms, from the virtuosity of the nouveau roman and *Finnegans Wake* to the imbecile gimmickry of cut-ups. At the other, in the production line of lively reportage, distant short-winded descendants of the comedy of manners.

The old order of fiction is past, and the new arises – with new answers. Or does it? That remains to be looked into.

I distrust the word *alienation*. It turns up in as many contexts as commitment and authenticity and unnumbered other slippery terms. But there is nothing evidently absurd in the Marxist argument that the novel may not be able to survive in any significant form – even as part of a literature of protest – in a society which no longer feels wholehearted respect for the values its architects took for granted. A society suffering from boredom with meaningless repetitive work, distaste for the cancerous growth of bureaucrats, bewilderment about its future, is little likely to inspire or welcome a contemporary *Middlemarch* or even an *Old Wives Tale*, though it may welcome with relief any intelligent eccentric able to provide a new aesthetic sensation, provided it is intelligible, or with indulgence the torrent of jack-in-the-box talent.

It is arguable – what can one not argue, given the example of historicists? – that the landscape the novelist is forced to move in has become so depersonalised or dehumanised by the traffic of machines, mechanised entertainment, learning, industry, transport, art, that he can no longer draw nourishment from a community which once supported him by its mere familiar existence, even when its attitude to his work was indifferent or hostile. The writer of centuries before ours was not, in today's sense of the word, alienated. He might elect to live on the margin of society, a reprobate, a *vagus*, he might be defeated in his ambitions by poverty and lack of brute energy. But his work drew on the same vital sources that nourished his fellows. The age of Chaucer and Langland lay under the threat of plague and famine, but the rivers of the mind and spirit were rising again in Europe. The age of the Elizabethan and Jacobean writers was cruel enough, filthy and unjust enough, but its life ran at high tide. Our age is running against us: it makes us no promises we can trust, offers us no certain future. We write against its pressure, or we add our work to its anguish, its dryness, its social and existential fears.

Suppose for a moment that we are trapped in the nihilism Nietzsche saw coming, suppose that the only world common to us all is the world of the nuclear menace, racial and ideological conflict, and the abyss of incomprehension and mistrust between the generations?

(In Europe we are still some way from the vision of a possible future I came on in a description of an Indian factory village: men and women housed in rows of windowless cement cubicles built along an open drain flushed two or three times a day to get rid of excreta; others living in blocks of cells, irrigated daily, three human objects to a cell; doorways but no doors, a communal kitchen and eating-room. A nightmare and a mocking mirror image of one aspect of our society. What is the essential difference between these cells and the blocks of flats going up in all western countries, the high point of impersonal efficient living? Obvious differences, but are they essential? Or is this factory village any one of these rectangular blocks reduced to its poorest barest model, without benefit of the screens we more delicate souls put up against sweat, ordures, bodily promiscuity? You reject the thought, but are you sure? Are you sure of being able to avoid a future in which nothing will be made slowly and thoughtfully by hand, neither bread nor art, and only a privileged élite and a dwindling handful of half-starved primitives have room to be private?)

Since neither Marx nor his disciples foresaw what twists human nature would give his doctrine in societies where it was put into effect, can we accept blindly that the Marxist critic understands, profoundly, the effects of social and economic revolution even on the superstructures of society, including the novel? The eccentricities and invalidism of fiction in our day are – perhaps – undeniable. Open to debate at least, in a day when an apparently sane man asks for a random heap of semi-literate pages to be accepted as a novel.

The Marxist diagnosis, rational so far as it goes, does not go far enough. It ignores, more commonly finds it easier and comfortable to denature, the intentional creative impulse of the writer, conceived and quickened at a depth below his susceptibility to social pressures, and not to be conjured away by the simple trick of calling it the 'Intentional Fallacy'. Hence what it offers us is a sensible and partial analysis, like saying of a broken marriage: It broke down because the two people involved were poor and bored. The question remains open: Why did poverty and boredom have *this* effect on them?

*

Yet another diagnosis – lest I offend the austere shade of Julien Benda I won't call it philosophical – traces the root of the novel's decline to the treacherous betrayal of reason, to a mistrust of reason and the rational consciousness, a rejection of the intellect as the only or finest tool of understanding. This rejection, mistrust, suspicion, call it what you please, did not begin with Hitler and his order of the day 'not to seek out objective truth so far as it may be favourable to others, but unceasingly to serve one's own truth', which, if it had triumphed, would have drowned civilisation in what D. H. Lawrence called 'the grand sea of the living blood'. It did not begin with the seductive philosophy of Bergson. Nor with Freud's night journey through the Unconscious. It has as many roots as bindweed: one of them is Hegelian, to be pulled up out of the *Grundlinien der Philosophie des Rechts*. It displays symptoms of a reaction. Against what? Against the defiant delight with which Renaissance art broke ecclesiastical bounds, against the ferocious energy with which Rembrandt seized the intellect of the viewer and ordered him to *see*? This lively supremacy of the intellect endures, through all changes of visual experience, down to the great nineteenth-century French painters, down to Cézanne, with an ever increasing stress on the artist's own conscious energy as the focus for admiration, down to a con-

33

summation or natural death in non-representational art and its all but exclusive interest in *process*.

Not *pari passu* – the arts never keep the same time – literature was following a somewhat like road, to reach as self-assertive a cry: *Madame Bovary, c'est moi.*

Such a degree of self-consciousness could not be further exploited. There had to be a reversal of energy, or a break-through. To say that Freud provided it is no more and no less a half-truth than most of the facts of history, including the history of literature.

The most prodigious, and therefore the most revealing, break-through was made by the Surrealists. Their writing be-came, or tried hard to become as uncontrolled, as anti-intel-lectual, as their writing about it relied on rational language. The most intelligent and sensitive of critics, Herbert Read, ex-plained in 1936 that 'it is only now, with the aid of modern dialectics and modern psychology, in the name of Marx and Freud, that poets and painters have found themselves in a position to put their beliefs on a scientific basis, thereby initiat-ing a continuous and deliberate creative activity whose only laws are the laws of its own dynamics.' Elsewhere he said, 'The paradox of such conscious control being that its aim is to cir-cumvent the intellect, the normal instrument of conscious con-trol,' leaving us bewildered in front of a process which can only be described as the intellect circumventing itself.

Other, less intelligent, more actively practising Surrealists gave other definitions. '. . . we know that the surrealist text is a complete submission to the automatism of thought, that the spirit hears its own unconscious voice and that the poet tran-scribes without the intervention of the controlling reason.' (Georges Huguet.)

I mistrust a doctrine that begins by asking the intellect to circumvent itself. It is true enough that the impulse to write starts in subliminal depths. The greater the writer the more boldly he moves about there. The degree of his success as a writer is the degree to which he contrives to disengage himself from this unconscious mass of feelings, words, images, to draw back from it, far enough to be in a fit state to present it in coherent intelligible form. By relating a great many images to one another, by concentrating a great many feelings into one, he gives form and substance to vast tracts of our common human experience. The effort involves him in becoming more passionately attentive, more conscious, not more automatic. This is true even though part of the process called 'exerting attention' takes place subliminally. There is an unconscious and a conscious attention at work. Both are essential to the writing of a novel.

I did not intend to write the last few paragraphs. Without intending it I have been trying to please a half-maliciously half-ironically smiling shade, that of the author of *La trahison des clercs*. What I intended was no more than to speculate on the part the revolt against reason has played in a decline of the novel attested by so many distinguished judges. More particularly, on the effect on the novel of the overwhelming interest, sometimes rational and critical, sometimes ignorant, ill-informed, a child fumbling with a complex tool he does not understand, in the so-called unconscious.

One of the paradoxical side-effects of Freud's genius is that theories which could have developed only in a solid bourgeois milieu, and in fact were developed by an austere moralist, have helped on the disintegration of society and consequently of the novel. When, by keeping one eye resolutely shut, we learned to lay the blame for our failures and mental deformities on our parents, to say of our misdeeds: It wasn't I, it was the complex they planted in me, we not only made antic hay of notions of personal responsibility and dignity, but knocked from under the novel and drama their firmest prop, and by substituting involuntary tics for the myth of fate and character, let loose in them a species of anti-hero made to delight an analyst and fill critics' mouths with pebbles of jargon. There is a sense in which it is true that ideas are precipitated emotions: it is at this stage of crystallisation that they are part of the bone structure of the novel. Not in the raw. If Shakespeare had been moved to illustrate a complex, *Hamlet* would have dwindled to the puppetry of *Mourning Becomes Electra* and heaven knows how many clever interesting exercises in psychoanalysis masquerading as novels.

To measure at a glance the extent of the collapse, compare Stendhal's portrait of an outsider with Camus's Meursault. Both young men give way to irrational impulses, but Julien Sorel acts, and tries to kill, from motives he and his creator can on reflection grasp. He is a problematic character but not a projection of flickering moods. The language of the two novels reflects accurately the climate of the society in which each was written. Both writers are lucid, economical, dry, but Stendhal's language has no cloudy sediment, it conveys his intellectual and emotional knowledge of his chosen hero with absolute assurance and absolute clarity, where Camus evokes an ambiguous unease, suggests latent inexpressible emotions, and leaves us with an undisclosed, unassimilated, possibly unassimilable meaning, personal to the writer, born of his sense of being threatened, from within and without, by moral and social forces not in his control.

I am not sure what it has profited us, either as writers or as social beings, to turn rejection of our parents – a sound natural effect of our helplessness as children, which vanishes, or should do, when we enter into life and can afford to think with pity and indulgence of the hypocritical pontiffs who darkened our infancy – into a solemn creed. The young author of a book predictably called *Bomb Culture* explains that: 'What is happening is more an evolutionary convulsion than a reformation.

Young people are not correcting society. They are regurgitating it.'

To say that the few novels so far thrown up by the convulsion are negligible is mildly unjust to one or two. But it is not unjust to speak of an anti-literature, plumped out with clichés, ritual abuse (of aged hypocrites and philistines), fragments of perished ideologies, mindless violence, talk-fests of astonishing vacuity, the sub-culture of pop in all its forms. The belief that self-discipline is the worst of evils, that nothing is so important as to vent our feelings, so unaffected, so bold, so like eagles renewed, would have struck me in my straitened, idol-breaking, sometimes hungry youth as too silly to be true. Dionysius, scurvily bearded, in tatty garments, is a pathetic figure. And, in so far as he concerns himself with his own needs, emotions and experiences to the virtual exclusion of everything else, humanly and aesthetically speaking a dead loss.

It is not I, it is my young self who feels nothing but contempt for that fraction of a generation which needs drugs to heighten, as the jargon goes, its perception. With the whole of the world in front of you – books not read, paintings not seen, music not heard, foreign cities not visited – how in pity's name can you waste time in mindless peace or ecstasy? Drugs should be for the old, who have lost the use of their minds and bodies. The idea of the Romantics that there is a direct connection between the artist and sickness, disease, derangement of the senses, may very well be true. It scarcely applies to an adolescent with no more talent than he needs to live by. Moreover, the supremely talented have always used their disease, not been used by it.

Perhaps it is a pity that great intellects discredited the ancient images of religion so thoroughly without taking the precaution to provide some other handhold for the immaturity of the race. So few of us – how intimately I know it – are by nature gentle, charitable, graceful, honest, clear-sighted, reasonable.

God, the intellect, reason – but not, alas, the doctrinaires, murderers on principle – were all pulled from their high place at about the same time, if not by the same impulse. Even more passionately than the men of the Enlightenment, the thinkers of the Victorian age revered Reason, and nothing is more derisible than a fallen idol. There are respectable grounds for its disgrace: reason divorced from imagination devised the gas-chambers, and how, without sophistry, condone the use of the intellect to invent napalm? None the less it is a shade too irrational to suppose that the answer to all our problems, social and individual, is emotion regarded *as a substitute* for order and, alas, grammar.

*

Among all the reasons its critics advance for the novel's poor health is one it is impossible to brush aside, and as impossible not to respect. It is that the world today is not so much too complex for a novelist to interpret as too abysmally, too unmanageably, vile. Tolstoy and Stendhal could observe war calmly, with compassion, irony, brotherly respect, and in later more devastating wars it was still possible for a few novelists, an Arnold Zweig, a Malraux, a Frederick Manning, to match in depth and energy the narratives of survivors. But what novelist can summon irony and serene understanding to help him resolve the facts of Buchenwald, Mauthausen, Auschwitz, Treblinka, and all the other places of torture and killing which in our day filled Europe with the stench of a cruelty beyond forgiveness? It is a question of understanding and explaining the least explicable – ultimately inexplicable – acts of a man's life, including the acts of torturers. Can human beings turn into literature what is wholly inhuman? Our world is one in which, *knowing what they did*, sane commonplace officials drove millions of men, women, children, into gas-chambers to die in agony of body and mind, sane civil servants organised the delivery of these poor creatures of flesh and blood to their butchers. *This* reality, the reality of life and death in the extermination camps, is strictly incommunicable. Partly incommunicable as fact, even by the survivors, will it ever be communicable as fiction?

A writer can report what sears the mind to read – one's mind is scarred forever by David Rousset's *Les jours de notre mort*, by *The Warsaw Diary of Chaim Kaplan*. Can he incarnate it? Any novelist living now would have to overcome more than the difficulty of giving imaginative expression to the reality behind the bare records. He would have to overcome a certain shame at touching them, a little as if he were bending over one of the pitiful heaps of garments, children's shoes, false teeth, in the death camps, and taking something for his own use.

Brought face to face with a common agony, a novelist, like a painter, has two ways open to him: he can turn it into an abstraction, as Picasso did in *Guernica*, or make the acutely more difficult effort, made by Goya, to evoke the living human image of fear, anguish, violent death. It is conceivable that, generations from now, a Stendhal turning the pages of old newspapers and contemporary records will be able to feel calmly that in a massacre the death of a single man is supremely significant, and be moved to try to penetrate the thoughts and emotions of an Eichmann, or of a Jewish father hanging his young son in the camp barracks to save him from being tortured again, or of the mother of the Vietnamese child dying as a child dies of napalm burns.

This future novelist is thinkable because we can say that he has existed. By a freakish miracle, a Jew born in Prague in 1883, and dying in 1924, was able to give a voice and face, even a smiling face, to our irredeemable disgrace before it happened.

39

Like a blind man palping the face he cannot see, Kafka evoked from his own rejection – by orthodox fellow-Jews and Gentile fellow-countrymen – a ghostly foreknowledge of the total rejection of the Jew in Europe between 1933 and 1945, thrust out of humanity to become an object. The object of hatred or of a cold curiosity like that of the Nazi official watching the convulsive struggles of the gassed through a spy-hole in the oven wall.

The information his sensitive finger-tips brought him was ambiguous. It took too many forms, on too many levels. He was acutely aware of the growing uncertainties of the ordinary man, his sense of being frustrated, coerced, belittled, in a bureaucratic society. On a lower level he discovered in himself that his innocence does not save the outcast from the torments of guilt: the infant feels guilty *because* he is slapped, the justifiably rebellious son is guilty of disappointing the father who oppresses him, the K. of *The Trial* becomes guilty after he is accused of a never formulated crime. On the lowest darkest level of all, he knew, with pitiless lucidity, that, guilty of having been born, he had been sentenced to die, 'like a dog.' Like the child his mother carries naked as a worm into the gas-chamber.

The fact that with this knowledge in his veins he was able to write about terror and despair in a clear imaginatively ordered way, lets me expect with a little confidence the birth, after the necessary recoil in time, of a future Stendhal. So be we have a future . . .

3. Language: a digression

In the beginning was the Word. But it was not the beginning. The moment when speech began, suddenly or imperceptibly, to evolve from the animal grunts and signs that were enough for a remote ancestor of ours marks, across an unimagined gap, a beginning. We live, on this side of the gap, lives defined, determined in root and essence, by language. Beliefs, customs, political structures, habits, values, speculations, metaphysics, the great ecclesiastic's idea of God and the unexacting notions of reality recorded by any one of today's novelists, derive from the words in which, only in which, we experience them. The greater novelist is distinguished from his dwarfish fellows by his superb capacity to feel and to feel in words: at a farther stage words breed words in his mind and shape his experience. Even the fascinating and difficult advance in linguistics is bounded by its explorers' involvement in words; the field they work in is as full of voices as Prospero's isle.

A novel is in one of its aspects its moment in time, signalled by the metaphysical smell its language gives off. An old gardener I knew as a child, who had been blind since the age of eight, could tell not only the state of health of a plant by smelling its leaves and stems but the precise stage of growth and decay it had reached. So, a piece of writing gives its situation in a society away to an alertly patient reader by a sublanguage below the words. Place side by side two equally erotic passages from an eighteenth-century writer and the author of *An American Dream*, and a single reading is enough to place each in its historical moment and to let the reader, like the old blind gardener, guess how close it is to disintegrating.

From the supreme cathedrals of philosophy to the newest jerry-built novel, literature springs out of the collision between reality and language, between a writer's intimate sense of himself and society and himself in society, and the impossible attempt to squeeze the whole of it into the words available to him. In the instant he sits down to write he forgets that it is impossible. If he could not forget it he could not write, not even a novel.

The language of the fiction writer is determined by the peculiar nature of his original impulse. Any novelist who is more, even only a little more, than an impostor, a faker, does not offer a copy of the world. He is not being moved by the wish to imitate – Tolstoy did not offer an imitation of Russian social and family life, nor Joyce an imitation of life in Dublin. His impulse is to create, through language, a rival world (an effort which paradoxically involves him not in creating a beautiful or ugly illusion, a lie, but in dissipating illusion to reveal the world in which the human will and passions act). His world is simultaneously a vision and a language. It begins its existence in the words which stand for it in his mind.

It is quite possible for a writer to accept, sincerely, a critical doctrine of his novel as an imitation of reality. He may never know that it began with the mysterious rising, at an obscure depth, of those heavenly twins, the word and the image, which is as far back as he can trace his impulse. But he behaves as if he knew. At this deepest level, words and vision are inseparable, as are body and spirit in the acts of the living man.

No matter into what form the novelist shapes his vision, lyrical, symbolist, neo-naturalist, any, the language is an involuntary confession of social and moral attitudes and intentions, and an explicit criticism of them through his sensibility, his hard effort to explore them with an always more acute and sceptical eye, and still harder effort not to betray the vision by a failure – at some level, some stage in his journey – in communication.

I cannot be interested by a world seen as a tripper sees it, without giving himself the pains to make human sense of it. The world of any novel worth reading – or worth my reading, considering how little time I have left – is on one level the Double of a portion of reality the novelist attended to with sensual rage and fiercely directed mental energy. Hence my ineradicable certainty that to write about our incoherent world in a wilfully incoherent style is clumsy and stupid. Why should I give myself the trouble of reading a novelist who is as exasperated and baffled as I am by the spectacle of a world bedevilled by a technical explosion that no political, social, religious or aesthetic creed is strong enough to control? If he can't impose order on his experience, he is little less of a barbarian than the industrialist who builds a skyscraper in front of a cathedral or the BBC official who sites a television mast beside the ruins of a Benedictine abbey: the difference between them is only that it has not yet occurred to industrialist or official to justify his barbarism by identifying it with aesthetic boldness.

Genius may be a divine sickness, but a writer in a frenzy is a bore. What a manufactured incoherence conveys is not a vision of chaos, not a vivid apprehension of it, but a sense-deadening and mind-blurring noise. One communicates something, certainly, by screaming, stammering, making disordered gestures, rolling on the floor, frothing at the mouth like an epileptic, but less than by keeping control of one's mind and tongue. The calm pages in which, in *La condition humaine*, Malraux narrates the last minutes of the prisoners thrown alive into the boiler of a locomotive sear like ice, as do the laconic sentences Stendhal uses to describe an atrocious act. In contrast, the murderous quarrel between father and son in Celine's *Mort à credit*, praised by a great critic for its sickening power, is reminiscent chiefly of Micky Spillane. And this is true of the bawling tone resorted to by novelists as worthy of respect as Günter Grass: they make an effect but it is a botched effect. The portrait of an idiot is less powerfully drawn by imitating his actual gestures and speech than by seeing them reflected in the mind of a sane person who loves him: what in a human being or in society is irretrievably incoherent needs, to be grasped in its fullest absurdity or horror, is a measuring rod, a *point d'appui* in coherence. How else can you judge it?

We have been misled by the notion of the novelist as a camera-eye into supposing that a truly honest picture of the collapsing world we live in will emerge from collapsed sentences. The camera itself, even the television camera, cheats, showing us the distorted face but not the thoughts passing behind it, perhaps only thoughts of a street corner or a piece of new bread. It is true that language itself cheats: words never convey the whole of an experience, not even the simplest. But if all that the novelist conveys of his experience of violence and disorder is the look of it and the confused noises, he might as well drop his pen and leave me to stare at the television set. What I want from him is not the face of that old woman stooping over the bombed-out ruin of her house, but what is passing through her mind in the moment when she runs a caressing hand over a cracked cup. To be conveyed, if at all, in words which have been chosen and put into her mouth by the writer for their ironic significance, for their hint of what, in the last resort, reconciles a human being to going on living. And by finding other words to evoke the gesture – of affection, memory, regret – made by the worn fingers with their work-swollen knuckles.

Within the limits of a finely-organised, even rigid control, the novelist can let himself admit to the most insane passions, the most heretical, subversive, vile, shocking ideas, the absolute in despair or ecstasy, without his work becoming a verbal evacuation. I am unable to forgive a bore who has neither the discipline nor the manners to make sense of his emotions before asking me to attend to them.

Wilful sabotage of coherence does worse than bore me. I believe coldly that Joyce did literature a disservice by the skill, persistence, courage, with which in *Finnegans Wake* he laboured to disintegrate language. Language is one of the thin walls humanity has built up over centuries against its own bestial and destructive impulses, against the very impulse that in a few days in 1944 destroyed all the great libraries of Warsaw. With one half of my mind I admire Joyce the great sculptor of language, the great experimenter, with the other I see him as the nihilist making a world in which there are no credible imperishable meanings, no humane or rationally accepted values at all.

There are less serious aspects of the collapse of language. Sad, but not serious. It is sad that a mass of lively and sometimes intelligent novels crumbles and sinks into the ground in a few years or, more likely, a few months, because they were fabricated – pre-fabricated – of half-effaced words, as if their authors had said to themselves: All is going to collapse any minute, think of the bomb, think of the decay of religion, chastity, the family, think of the reverence paid to popular entertainers, of the four solemn wireless bulletins put out when a Beatle's tonsils are removed, of reputable journalists extolling pretty young women in a tone more suited to Mary Magdalene: dishevelled writing best fits a dishevelled age.

It is astonishing into what high and highly respected levels of literature the worm makes its way. Kenneth Burke is a critic with an immense and justified reputation for acumen and learning: I almost closed his *Philosophy of Literary Form* unread when, in the Preface, I stumbled over the sentence: 'The quickest way to sloganize this theory is to say that it is got by treating the terms "dramatic" and "dialectical" as synonymous.' To sloganize! It is not possible, I thought, that a man who uses this

45

language can be a writer with any feeling for words or integrity as a thinker. Every association of the word 'slogan' is with propaganda or advertising: how could he let them echo through his invented – did he invent it or only put a careless hand on it? – verb? Not literature alone, but society itself is wormed and rotten when language ceases to be respected not merely by advertisers and politicians, but by persons of learning and authority.

On one of its levels language is a translation of our experience into images – indeed, on many levels, from the casual transformation of an object into a verbal image – *I was rooted to the spot, I burned with shame* – to the unfolding coils of metaphor in a page of Proust's. Its rough and ready handling by novelists as clever as A. and B. creates a sort of moral confusion in their readers' minds by blurring the complex sense of the image. It may be that they don't know for whom they are writing and can rely on no clear response: they lack even the assurance of François Mauriac or Graham Greene that an idiom of their thought will be familiar to a great many people. Instinctively they use a reach-me-down idiom in the hope of being widely understood, and pay with shallowness of meaning and a short life for their immediate success. (But sometimes a passing target is hit full in the centre, as in *Lucky Jim*, and the mark made lasts a perceptible time.)

None of this has anything to do with plainness and everyday speech. The plainness of Bunyan, laid on him, is a translucent river carrying easily depth on depth of allusion, to interior events of the greatest importance. The difference between him and A. and B. is that yawning between a writer who handles words with respect for their precision and dangerous ambiguity and another who does not care how defaced and greasy they are so long as they pay his fare.

Why, if his sharpest wish is to catch as many ears as possible with his cleverness, pungent wit, readability, rib-tickling humour and bold opinions should a novelist spend time and energy to translate sensations and perceptions into the most exact, most evocative words, time and energy more profitably spent to write another lively scene? Why indeed?

This is not the way to put it. If, like Stendhal, he had spent years registering, studying, botanising the slightest movements of feeling, his own and other men's, before sitting down to write a novel, he could be lucid and subtle *and* quick. In a single jet, between the 4th of November and the 26th of December, Stendhal wrote or dictated the whole of the *Chartreuse de Parme*, that Mozartian masterpiece, but he drew it from the rich veins of a life lived with a pitiless eye on himself – without sparing the animal, he said – and with a total lack of worldly prudence. Which of us has that courage and self-disregard?

It is fallacious to talk about the writer's use of language as if style were no more than technique and faithful practice. It is that, but in the second place. First of all, it is the man who feels and observes: the quality of his work depends most intimately on his capacity to rejoice and suffer, on the acuteness and patient accuracy of his mind's eye. His choice of words to convey what he sees and has endured, critically important as it is, is largely instinctive, a question of the inner ear, given him or not given him.

Why do I write this with reluctance? I think because it seems to deny or deprecate the truly exquisite pleasure I get out of a search for the precise (concrete, subtle, fluid) word. I can spend an hour on a word or a phrase. Who will notice it? Who cares? No one, two or three persons. But I have been madly happy for an hour.

It is anything but fallacious to think that the increasing disintegration of language reflects or rehearses a social breakdown. But the argument leaves out too much. An English writer is *in* his language as he is in the country that bred him.

47

His freedom of movement in it is shackled by prohibitions and intimations beyond his control, but he can choose freely to live in it in bohemian squalor, or iu urbane and possibly mannerist formality, or as an alert labourer in a familiar long-used field. No doubt the reason why he is moved to write continually about, say, incest, or treachery, is a biological one, to be discovered if anywhere in his first secret impulses, but he acquired his range of technical, intellectual, moral habits later, in his green years as writer. He chooses consciously whether to use his verbal tools as a hardworking craftsman, as a careless or ignorant amateur, as one of God's spies, as a priest, as a show-off 'cavorting and curvetting like a bloody peacock', as what you will, tenderly or harshly, gaily, humbly moved by love or hate of his kind. He did not choose his inherited estate of language, he labours or cavorts in a pre-formed labyrinth. He can choose only among words that have been used again and again, every one of them a reservoir of coded memories. Since not a word rises to the surface of his mind which is not weighted by the feelings and speculations of centuries of spoken and written English; since each he touches vibrates with echoes going back to the birth of his mother tongue, the effort to use them in a new way – if he has the rare impulse to make it – is doomed to a measure of failure. Words lie to him continually or shamleessly. He can ignore ambiguities, or, as Joyce did, exploit them, but not purge them.

One has the awful sense, reading A. and B., that they have no ear, and the most impoverished sensibility, like a piano with missing keys or a single-stringed fiddle. It is unreasonable, even indecent, to blame the victims of a defective ear. But I am not obliged to carry forbearance of a natural defect to the point of being indifferent to it. If I no longer have the heart to read a page of their novels, it is not because they might not interest me, but because I cannot stomach the dead flat language. Fumbling through the worn coins in their hands, they write:

I had sex. Or: I went into Juliet's bedroom and screwed her. Dead clichés, nothing to do with the living processes of literature.

It may be that the custom of sitting down to type your novel rather than write it encourages slovenliness. Writing by hand exacts from the brain a more intimate effort, slower, giving time for second thoughts.

No one would deny that the novelist's situation is more uneasy now than it was before he had to compete for attention in a society provided with so many more immediately exciting entertainers. Obviously, the writer who wants to sell himself in a crowded mass market cannot approach it as he might a man sitting over a book he has all the time in the world to meditate. The younger and more impatient he is, the quicker he will be to realise that catching the eye of an audience used to brightly-packaged goods is an affair of other methods than those used by his long-winded predecessors. Very naturally, his first impulse is to strip off the traditional novelist's morning coat or dressing-gown, make his points without too much subtlety, laugh, tell intimate little stories, fill pages with the minute particulars of living or inanimate objects, bring on new figures, the unreconstructed young rebel, with or without his psychiatrist, the gay unwashed and uncareful, and now and then say something moving, or drop a paragraph which shows that he, too, has his moments of deep feeling. Or cover his nakedness with a sketchy symbolism, like the young narrator of a recent novel (forethoughtfully laid in a trawler) who vomits continually, his memories and his meals.

What is wrong with that? Why, nothing. Except that it is not the peculiar task of the imaginative writer. It calls on his wits, but not for what he alone can offer, and in the great age of the novel thought himself compelled and competent to offer, a vision of human nature caught between the furies of its instincts and the pitiless dynamics of society.

49

'Sensibility,' said Eliot, 'alters from generation to generation in everybody, whether we will or not: but expression is only altered by a man of genius.' He did not add that it can be altered for the worse very rapidly, in a generation or two, without the intervention of genius, given a certain degree of social and psychological tension, of loss of confidence in the future, in the continuance of what, timidly or ironically, we still speak of as the humanities or the essential decencies. My complaint of A. and B. is not that they feel in a disturbingly new way about moral and aesthetic conduct, ideals, obligations, but that their new sensibility, such as it is, is expressed in a prose so slipshod and loose-textured, so innocent alike of hard thinking and grammar, that it conveys very little worth the cost of carriage. In the end, one doubts whether they have anything new or disturbing in their heads.

They are not important. They are terribly important. Vigorous fast-growing weeds, they cumber the ground, a sub-culture of massive extent, exhausting the soil, suffocating plants of slower or more difficult birth. Varied in their secondary characteristics, they none the less belong to a common order, and for all their vigour, and, at times, charm, they are infected by the common ailments and vices of mass media. As urgently as televised shows they must make their point quickly and at all costs, they cannot afford the reckless expense of time needed to dig to the roots of an experience. Nor must they be far out of the reach of a lowest common measure of intelligence.

In this testing climate, talented and in their way serious writers become well-set machines for turning out sound (arresting, powerful, witty, moving) products, instantly enjoyed and quickly replaced out of stock. It is no impoliteness to a score of successful artisans, gratified by praise and attention and destined to sink without trace when, or before, they die in the flesh, to say that their understanding of the relations of men and women with each other and with society is conveyed to a mass audience in a competent or lively and above all easily-read prose, where D. H. Lawrence, who really had something new to say about these, a new insight, needed – and laboured to achieve and in his finest novels (which do not include *Lady Chatterley's Lover*) did triumphantly achieve – a prose of extreme subtlety and nervous energy, impossible to take in at a single reading and impossible to accommodate inside a species of mass culture which comes close to being no culture at all.

When language is impoverished all is impoverished. At best, words distort and partly betray the truths they make visible. At worst, when they are used sluttishly, with no care to fit them to a reality penetrated as deeply as the writer's intellect, good faith, and above all energy, will take him, they weaken still further the most critical of all links with the past and future of our common culture, and add to the chaos and unhappiness of our time.

4. The novel as an art form

The sensuous pleasure to be had from the contemplation of art, any work of art, is inextricably twisted with the stirrings of intellectual curiosity – What does this mean? What does it mean to me? What did its creator mean? – which can be mischievous, even malignant, but, the human brain being what it is, a two-handed engine for enjoying and analysing, it must be allowed for. We experience art sensually and in the same breath accept from it some kind of information. A great novel can stand a devil of a lot of questioning and analysing unharmed, and the others do not matter. The serious mischief begins when form and content are thought of as separable components of the work, with marks awarded to Tolstoy for content (insight into human nature, knowledge of society, and so on and so forth), and to Henry James or Robbe-Grillet for formal graces, on a sliding scale determined by the critic's temperament or prejudices.

To draw a distinction between the novel as a picture of reality and as a manifestation of the writer's craftsmanship is finally illusory. Inevitably it is both, and which aspect of the single phenomenon is considered at any moment the more important is ultimately a social choice, largely determined by the writer's attitude to his world.

The fastidious rejection by a few writers, novelists and poets, of the values of nineteenth-century bourgeois society began when that society was still confidently enriching itself. But the first impulse of a responsible writer is not to turn against form conceived in words. He turns to it. He devotes himself to its

52

problems, like a saint to his faith, like St Gustave, behaving much as a cultivated man, suspecting that he is mortally sick, may take pains to live as a dandy.

In the novels of Tolstoy and George Eliot, form is the necessary instrument of content: many differences of temper but little or no inclination to suppose that the novel had any more important business than the creation of characters caught in a social web. The separation, in the writer's, then in the critic's and the reader's mind, of form from content had the effect of making form an object, to perfect which the writer toiled with passion and a sense of priestly duty. In Flaubert's hands form became the hieratic clothing of a vestal virgin. Later on, at a later stage in the process of objectifying form, it became, sometimes, the wrappings of a mummified body, as it does in certain nouveaux romans, when the content is frozen into immobility to allow it to be craftily manipulated.

During the last half-century critical concern with the novel as *first of all* a work of art has become common form. There was a period when Henry James was the only accredited guide to the composition of works qualifying, by the purity of their form, as art – works of art as distinct from 'such large loose baggy monsters' as *War and Peace*. A trying period for those who found irrational or old-maidish a definition of the serious novel which exalted that admirable work *The Portrait of a Lady* above *Anna Karenina*.

Less tedious, because revealing a geological shift in the aesthetic ground, is the insistence that 'the basic unit for contemporary art is not the idea, but the analysis and extension of sensations . . . The most interesting works of contemporary art (one can begin at least as far back as French symbolist poetry) are adventures in sensation, new "sensory mixes". Such art is, in principle, experimental – not out of an élitist disdain for what is accessible to the majority but precisely in the sense that science is experimental.' (Susan Sontag.)

53

Apart from the obligatory – and meaningless – genuflexion before science, this is not a new doctrine and has respectable ancestors. In 1896, Rémy de Gourmont was writing: 'La seule excuse qu'un homme a d'écrire c'est d'écrire lui-même, de dévoiler aux autres la sorte du monde qui se mire en son miroir individuel. Sa seule excuse est d'être originel; il doit dire des choses non encore dites, et les dire en une forme non encore formulée. Il doit se créer sa propre esthétique.'

Every novelist *s'écrit*, whether he is Flaubert or George Eliot or the author of the newest 'impressive first novel' or of the most 'distanced' of nouveaux romans. He writes out of his sensibility, intellect, genitals. The question is one of emphasis, of a shift in emphasis. On the whole, the great novels of the past have been written by men so possessed by a devouring interest in the world and man that the form they chose, and forced their vision into it, was of secondary concern to them. Or as if no novelist with the imaginative vitality to set himself the problems set by a *War and Peace*, a *Comédie humaine*, had energy to spare to attend to perfection of form, or – looking at it more closely – as if his passionate attention to his matter were simultaneously and unselfconsciously a passionate attention to setting it out. Or as if he felt intuitively that the novel conceived as spiritual witness to an age exacted a naked clarity, what Stendhal called an 'absence of style'. The single great exception to this rule – it is almost a rule – is a late one: his long novel, an indissoluble marriage between his dedicated effort to make profound sense of human life and the extreme intricacy and resonances of his manner, cost Proust his life, paid out day by day for more than seventeen years.

The modern novelist has lost the obsessive belief of a Balzac that he can animate a richly human world: instead he invites us to enter the frontier strip where he is the only native. He presents us with a fragment of reality in which he is intimately included, the thing perceived and the perceiving agent given equal importance in his mind. An involuntary impressionist, his guiding motive is the need to impose his experience, *sa petite sensation*. Far from disappearing into the structure of his work, his emotions and reflections stare at us from it, demanding to be noticed. Intelligently self-conscious or professionally self-exhibitionist, he rarely forgets himself in his creation, whether what he can exhibit is the genius of Montherlant – a brilliant comedian profoundly sure of his role and prepared at any moment to take the centre of the stage away from his characters – the acute social perception of one writer, or the delicate probing of personal relations of another. Or whether all he does is empty over an audience his private angers, frustrations, opinions, sexual needs, with varying degrees of skill and talent.

Instinctively we speak of 'Joyce's Dublin': it would not occur to us to say, 'Tolstoy's (or Pasternak's) Moscow'. But where in *Ulysses* the impulse towards a subtle form of self-indulgence is overborne by the desperate courage of Joyce's struggle to recall and pin down his Dublin, one face of the closed private world of *Finnegans Wake* wears the forbidding mask of an elaborate word game, starting up in readers an exalted form of the state of mind in which they approach a difficult crossword, and exacting a kind of admiration and wonder not exacted by less resolutely hermetic masterpieces.

I am not by nature ungrateful. It delights me to pay tribute to the many poignant evocations of personal sufferings and joys, thoughtful studies of homosexuals and unmarried mothers, of mental cases enduring the final privacy of madness, and – of course – that most modern of anti-heroes, the outsider. So far as the novel is concerned, this last has become the insider, the typical, the rule. Indeed, why not? Things fall apart, the centre cannot hold – and the rest of it and the rest of it. What quicker simpler way to forget the loss of social coherence than to sink oneself in analyses of private eccentricities?

There is abundance of talent, and worse ways of spending it than in adding to the yearly score of truly admirable, interesting (until one is too old to be easily interested) and expendable novels.

On its more lyrical side the impressionist novel, endemic in our time, has a natural tendency to slide closer to the other arts, most naturally and easily towards poetry and music. Long passages of Laurence Durrell's *Alexandria Quartet* give pleasure of the sort given by descriptive poetry and music. For Giraudoux, that novelist who was the dear companion of my younger heart and spirit for more years than I remember – I know his work better than do most of his countrymen – any human being, an inspector of weights and measures, a scientist, a young girl, an old dying statesman, becomes the excuse for the most enchanting poetic construction. No doubt, any minute now I shall discover that I am too old to re-read *Siegfried et le Limousin* or *Bella*. But not, but never, to eject thirty-six shabby volumes from my book-shelves, or make nothing of the years of happiness I owe him.

The weakness, the deep flaw, of the poetic novel is that it can never match the infinitely greater concentration of poetry. Lyric poetry springs out of the immediate seizing of a sensory or visionary experience. The true function of prose is to convey an apprehension of reality reached by reflective analysis and sustained thought. This is not to belittle, still less deny the vital role the novelist's senses play in the conception and execution of his work, but only to stress the direct part rational consciousness must play in what he makes of the information his senses offer him. A novel can be dismembered by critic or reader, and viewed in narrowly sociological, psychological, linguistic aspects, with loss of virtue, it is true, but with smaller loss than can a poem, which is utterly destroyed if torn apart into theme and style. At some point in the spectrum of prose writing, stretching from the most strictly controlled and most highly

organised language – that is, from the point where language
approximates most nearly to its control and organisation by a
poet or a great dramatist – to the more loosely organised
language of fiction, a qualitative shift takes place in the writer's
attention. The sharpest point of his attention shifts from his
manner to his matter, the human will, human passions, acting
and being acted on in society. In society. However withdrawn,
introverted, the novelist's creature, like God's, is inescapably
attached to society. The solitude even of a hermit or a mad-
man touches society at some turn between birth and death. To
depict only the hermit's religious and spiritual emotions issues
in theology or mysticism or poetry. To depict only the inner
world of any person demands either a psychological treatise or
the autonomy of poetry. The language of the novelist is not
simply more diffuse than the poet's, it is expository and dis-
cursive in essence. The form is merged with the conception,
the vision lived through the form, as properly as in poetry, but
on a different level. For the novelist, words are loaded in ways
to a degree that the poet, with his infinite licence to compress,
escapes. This does not imply that the prose of Tolstoy, of
Proust, is *not* a reorganisation, for their special purposes, of
everyday speech. It is to say that this reorganisation is a
secondary purpose of fiction, even of the greatest.

What, in the novel, is of first importance, is the energy,
emotional and intellectual, the writer brings to his experience
of life itself. His supreme impulse is his passion to feel and
know. The phrases he uses insist on being taken in the first
place in their precise meaning: the harmony, the gaiety, the
sense of tears in them, depend wholly on the skill with which
he relates them to each other in a succession which is not that
of poetry: he has not the licence of a poet to approximate his
language to music. The poetic novel is an attempt to insert
fiction in the spectrum at a point which draws it closer to
poetry and away from the strongest life of the novel. It can be,

often is, charming, intelligent, amusing. But it is a bastard minor art. The novelist's language cannot be autonomous: the closer it approaches to a sort of writing in which the image, the instrument of sense, becomes autonomous, the less defensible it is as prose, the less its raison d'être. Ideally the two disciplines should keep each other at a respectful distance, not allow the one to adulterate the other.

In its lowest form the hybrid called poetic prose is born of a morbid craving to inflate romantically the language of prose, an impulse very like that inciting market gardeners to grow marrows the size of sacks of wool, and as tasteless.

Poetic prose is not the same thing as a prose poem, strictly an effort to focus the reader's attention on an experience, possibly very small, which cuts straight down to the quick of an emotion or an idea. Kafka's *Auf der Galerie*, a prose poem if ever one was, is not written in poetic prose.

*

Strange hybrids are bred from the attempt to use words as a painter rightly uses colours or a composer sounds, to solve some problem in their relations. Gertrude Stein's verbal *pointillisme*, or Sartre's attempt in *Le Sursis* to orchestrate passages of the narrative by running two simultaneous events together in one sentence without benefit of punctuation, are laboratory experiments amusing for the writer – and for readers more genial, less easily bored, than I am.

The ear can pick up and merge the sounds of the instruments in an orchestra, a painting can establish itself in existence (only in existence) at a glance: using his own means, words following each other in time, the novelist can achieve aural complexity by, say, a cunning use of vowels, can evoke buried memories, his own or those of his race, setting off a depth charge of emotion, but – unless what he has to say is less important to him than its sound – he is forced to give voice to his thoughts in a succession of words and phrases, allowing his readers time to sort them out. Attempts to paint in words, or harmonise in words, have produced – as well as an absence of meaning – charming exciting approximations to *natures mortes* or impure (adulterated by the verbal echoes) sonatas. Only by a confusing of terms to be called novels. Why should a novelist compete with musician and painter in fields where they are at home and he only a clumsy intruder?

The dullest and most sterile form of the psychopathology of modern fiction, the surrealist novel, is mercifully rare – none of the novels of Raymond Queneau or Elias Canetti is in any sense surrealist: the Pataphysical humour and elusive bitterness of the first and the savagery of the second are in rational control from start to finish. I have said what I had to say about surrealism as an attack on the authority of reason, a limiting instance of that particular *trahison des clercs*. André Breton's Surrealist Manifesto of 1924 defined it, in paradoxically self-conscious rhetoric, as: 'Pure psychic automatism by which it is intended to express, either verbally or in writing, the true function of thought. Thought dictated in the absence of all control exerted by reason, and outside all aesthetic or moral preoccupation.' Reading it at the time, I did not believe that a sane and talented man had persuaded himself that the *true* function of thought is to evade rational control. Or that a premeditated madness and incoherence, however induced, is anything but a mocking negation of that function. Now I think it unlikely that either he or his friends and disciples had any intellectual interest in the paradox of totally irrational thinking. The whole movement, before it began to be explained and made the basis of solemn theses, was a gaily violent rebellion against established society, a great belly laugh issuing from millions of young bodies rotting in the war cemeteries of a Europe which had just destroyed itself. As such, I find it sympathetic – and, as well, a healthy evacuation, aesthetically all but sterile, intellectually a bore, and socially only tolerable if, when, it is fraudulent.

The Congo of the under-mind offers a superb jungle of images to the imagination of a painter. Translated directly into words, what it offers is a limitless possibility of distortion and counterfeit. All language distorts reality: to refuse even to try to control the distortions is frivolous at a deep level. Rejection of reason, submission to the voodoo of black humour, so-called automatic writing, the contemptuous impulse to disrupt the linguistic structure of human existence, all deeply frivolous, and finally deathly boring. ('La beauté sera convulsive ou ne sera pas,' Breton said, seemingly without reflecting how tedious convulsions become.) Need one take the surrealist writer seriously? Only on the ground that he dodges his double responsibility, as a writer, to find a meaning of sorts in life, whatever that meaning may turn out to be, *even a meaning of total non-sense and disaster.* Even to demonstrate that life is absurd exacts intelligible argument. Renouncing his responsibility to communicate, he not merely shuts himself in a private asylum, which he is free to do, but cuts the roots that descend unbroken, until he broke them, into a memory infinitely more vital to us than our little hoard of personal memories.

The novelist who writes out of a buried context of experience which the reader has no means of checking against his own is making things too easy for himself. (Come to that, what is easier, simpler, within the capacity of almost any age, any person, clever or stupid, educated or not, imaginative or not, than to arrange *la rencontre sur une table de dissection d'une machine à coudre et d'un parapluie*? The associations evoked by this anything but fortuitous assemblage are twitches of a willed unreason, a pre-arranged incoherence. Amusing? Oh, if you are easily amused.)

Years ago, a critic I respected deeply accused me, when I had made some comment on surrealist writing, of trying to damn a new growth. 'We can never,' he said angrily, 'draw back from an adventure, linguistic or plastic, into the future. We must face the incoherence and absurdity of our ephemeral lives. The insistence of the classic novelist on imposing meaning where none is has shut the novel into a strait-jacket inside which it is dying for want of exercise.' I was only momently abashed. I am not willing to advance into the future under the banner: Writers of the world unite, you have nothing to lose but control of your mind. If the novel is dying, I see no chance that dismembering it will revive it. Nor, coolly, that it is time yet to despair of the values of humanism.

We have lately been to the edge of an abyss of anti-human-ism and hallucinating madness. We shall never be far from it again. I take it to be no duty of the writer to advance into hell without, like Dante, taking along a classic guide.

To be of any aesthetic or human worth, fantasy exacts of its writer a better than nodding acquaintance with the real world. It exacts the control, the acute intelligence and profound gaiety of Jorge Luis Borges. Imitations I have read of *Ficciones* by an English novelist are so pallid that they disappear off the page. How can you fantasy a world you know so little about?

God be thanked, no novelist yet has been moved to attempt an equivalent of concrete poetry. Is it horribly possible that one will? It is. No sooner do we reflect that the nadir of silliness has been reached in an art, than something sillier shows its vacant face. I will take any odds that the first 'concrete' novel to find a publisher also finds a critic to herald it as 'inspiring and beautifully distanced'.

5. The nouveau roman: a new beginning?

The only way to enjoy the nouveau roman, or to meet it on the level and with the attention it merits, is to ignore the portentous theorising of its critics and adherents. No even casual glance at the exciting French scene can overlook it, but it is impossible to discuss it sensibly if it is regarded as a school, and not as the work of a number of writers as dissimilar as Alain Robbe-Grillet, Nathalie Sarraute, Michel Butor, Claude Simon, Robert Pinget, Philippe Sollers. It is manifestly irrational to approve or disapprove *en bloc* of writers who pursue intellectual and metaphysical ends which have little in common except an obsessive concern with technique and a conviction that the traditional novel is already stone dead. Only the barrier of a curiously humourless fanaticism lets them ignore the energy and perfect health of the later Jean Giono, Jean Cayrol, Louis Guilloux, Henry de Montherlant, and two or three others of their contemporaries. Perhaps, as resolute heretics, they avoid glancing at believers.

In France, even heresy rapidly hardens into dogma. That cherished in various sectarian forms among the new novelists has one root in the very respectable tradition going back at least to Flaubert. But since any withdrawal, even withdrawal into a life dedicated to technical mastery of an art, turns in on itself, what with Flaubert began as a cry of rage and contempt for the dehumanising pressure of bourgeois society has issued, in the hands of some later rebels, as a rejection of humanism. Not only does Robbe-Grillet ridicule our pathetic habit of humanising nature – or, as he prefers to say, 'contaminating' it (the word is loaded to give an effect of nausea) – by seeing our feelings reflected in it, the overcast sky grieving with us, the landscape enfolding, soothing, us. He condemns the fatuity of regarding the human creature as other than a bundle of impulses and sensations, an object among other objects, finally impenetrable, as are all objects. 'Ah, vous croyez encore,' he says mockingly, 'à la nature humaine, vous!' It is time to drop the illusion that man is the measure of all things. Torn adrift from his once privileged position in the universe, the human object appears in isolation, picked out like a detail, a hand, a profile, in a blown-up photograph of a painting. The Renaissance high tide of humanism has turned for good. (To the objection that this is against the nature of tides, unbelievers might retort that it never was a tide, it was an illusion brought on by looking too long at the exquisite labours of a few giants and at the last dazzling rays of light from classical Greece. Perhaps. But what a superb illusion.)

In any of its forms the nouveau roman places itself at the opposite pole to surrealism. The conscious intellect operates in it at every moment, on every level. One could even argue that it works too hard, interferes too strenuously, in the interests of a theory, with the novelist's freedom to create a viable world. Rejecting the concept of a stable reality, Claude Simon fixes his attention and that of his readers on the impersonal flux of matter, reflected in the all but endless twists and repetitions of his unconscionably long sentences. Robbe-Grillet's anxiety to purge his writing of anthropomorphic myths and illusions creates, less sharply than in his films, a world of precisely-described images, exciting or iterative distortions of reality. His rejection of rooted human values – and, naturally, of the novelist's duty to spell these out in sensuously living, articulate individuals – his denial or refusal of any possibility of genuine communication between human beings, imprisons the writer himself in the object. He isolates himself in it, or, like Nathalie

Sarraute, in the invisible movements of the sub-mind, them-selves objects.

L'homme est l'être qui ne peut sortir de soi, qui ne connaît les autres qu'en soi, et, en disant le contraire, ment. Proust, not Robbe-Grillet, said that. It is true – but the rule of conduct Robbe-Grillet draws from it as a writer leads him away from the man-centred world of the traditional novelist, the world not only of Tolstoy but of Proust and Joyce, towards the inhuman world of abstract art. The points of likeness between his aesthetic and that of the abstract painter are very clear. I realise that all my life I have been wrong in thinking of abstract art as a reflection of the impersonal dehumanising tendencies of our mechanised civilisation. It is not a reflection: it is a reaction, a flight into the farthest recesses of the self, a willed cult of in-wardness, the deliberate replacement of the body of the living world by the painter's arrogant reorganisation of it as an eviscerated statement of the relations between the signs made by line and colour. The novelist cannot carry solipsism so far. He can withdraw, in disgust, boredom, or fascinated self-hypnosis, into contemplation of the object, but not, since his tool is language, and words have a shifting life of their own and make too many complex signs, distort it beyond recogni-tion, or see nature coolly as 'uncontaminated'. In truth, for the writer, the world exists only as 'contaminated' by man: he 'contaminates' it by the very act of looking at it in order to describe it.

Nothing more natural than that the energies withdrawn from the classic novelist's effort to establish a person or group at the centre of a comprehensible world should turn towards a sharpened interest in technique. Natural, too, that this risks modifying the novel into an exercise in style, an intelligent effort to solve a set of finally insoluble equations. A world devoid of human meaning would be intolerably boring if there were no escape from it into some such difficult intellectual game. Robbe-Grillet's cerebral exercises can be exciting – everything for your amusement except a perspective of life. Or, as so often with Nathalie Sarraute, tedious: I know no more crashing bores in literature than Martereau and other skeletal characters of hers.

Like the revolution in music accomplished by Schoenberg, the nouveau roman offers the stimulus of a new sensory and intellectual experience, surprising, fascinating, or repellent and fatiguing. It has its spurious and doctrinaire side. The individual as writers have seen him since the time of Homer and the authors of the sagas does not become extinct when Robbe-Grillet says, 'The novel that contains characters belongs entirely to the past, it was peculiar to an age – that of the apogee of the individual.' What he is actually saying is: We know that the individual is not a person, he is a multiplicity of shifting I's. The task of discovering and translating into lucidly human terms some, the most persistent, most carefully hidden, or most compulsive of the motives that, turn and turn about, work in him is one I propose to dodge: instead, I shall give you a vivid pattern of physical images, as in a film, from which you may if you like deduce a reflection of the character; it will be as true and as false as any other. The responsibility for inventing it is yours, not mine.

As in an actual film, as in *L'année dernière à Marienbad*, what we are given is a shifting mosaic of images – gestures, inanimate objects, the movements of a hand or an insect, phrases repeated in changing contexts. The whole novel offers something of the peculiar dreaming pleasure of penetrating a looking-glass world. Ecstasy or nightmare, tragedy or comedy, enter it only to the extent to which a human being is allowed to take the centre of the stage, as in the novels that 'belong entirely to the past.' As in *Dans le labyrinthe*, where the lost feverish soldier dominates his surroundings. Phantasmal anguish, even if finally meaningless, is still the anguish of a person.

In the last resort it is not possible for the novelist to keep intact a belief in the indifference of the universe. Indifferent it no doubt is: the God who comforted Pascal has absconded, leaving man alone and faceless, an atom in a more or less organised vapour. If you like to think so. But certain of these atoms, Julien Sorel, let us say, or Anna Karenina, or Gwendolen Harleth or Mr Kurtz, are of infinitely more value as an object of my, the reader's, attention than the non-human objects competing with them for notice. The prolonged steady stare of a man, the directing energy of his mind, are what give the novel its value. Until it has been 'contaminated' by a man, the world is not fit matter for literature.

Nathalie Sarraute has her own self-conscious way of dealing with the difficulty – and final impossibility – of telling the truth about a human being, even the simplest. 'What I tried to show was certain "inner movements" by which I had long been attracted . . . These movements (*tropismes*), of which we are hardly cognisant, slip through us on the frontiers of consciousness in the form of undefinable extremely rapid sensations. They hide behind our gestures, beneath the words we speak and the feelings we manifest . . . They seemed, and still seem to me to constitute the secret sources of our existence . . . And since, while we are performing them, no words express them, not even those of the interior monologue – for they develop and pass through us very rapidly in the form of frequently very sharp brief sensations, without our clearly perceiving what they are – it was not possible to communicate them to the reader otherwise than by means of equivalent images that would make him experience analagous sensations . . .'

How did she write that without its crossing her mind that 'equivalent images' have been part of the novelist's battery of tools since the novel entered its classic period ? Indeed, speaking of the elder Karamazov's buffoonery in Father Zossima's cell, she says, 'all these disordered leapings and grimacings are the absolutely precise outward manifestations, reproduced without indulgence or desire to please . . . of these subtle, barely perceptible, fleeting, contradictory, evanescent movements, faint tremblings, ghosts of timid appeals and recoilings, pale shadows that flit by, whose unceasing play constitutes the invisible woof of all human relationships and the very substance of our lives.'

Can she believe that she has made a new discovery in noticing that our emotions are horribly sly and deceitful, made up of countless evasive impressions, sensations, images, memories, larval impulses, which slip through the finest net of language leaving traces fainter than those of a snail on a wall? Or that our actions lie about our motives? To tell us what a man did, what gestures he made, what expression crossed his face, may tell us little or nothing directly about the hidden determining movements of his being. These are strictly indescribable, taking their start below the roots of language. None the less, by delicacy and precision in his choice of words the writer is able to reflect these ghostly movements in action and dialogue, letting us guess at what we cannot see. In any event, it is the best he can do. His triumph, his stature as a writer, is measured by the length of time it takes us to think we have come to an end of one of his characters. Do you dare to say that you came to the end of Julien Sorel when his head rolled, or of Charlus after parting from him in his last palsied moments?

It may be that reality has to be flushed out of its burrow by patience and cunning. A sensation announces itself in the mind at a depth some way below intelligibility, to be pursued through successive disguises and approximations until it gives itself up in its real form. The scene involving Swann with the Duchesse of Guermantes and her red slippers is long and subtly articulate, and we see a great deal farther into both persons than we could ever have arrived at through a vapour of *tropismes.*

Ironically, Madame Sarraute's novels are more worth the trouble of reading them the nearer they approach to the old psychological novel, and the farther they retreat from her determination to suggest – in a prose reminiscent of the wavering reflection of an unseen water insect on the surface of a pond – the scarcely articulate 'sous-conversations' assumed to be going on continuously in all of us. Too often we are left with the boringness of the boring, whipping ourselves on with a memory of Dr Johnson – 'Why, Sir, if you were to read Richardson for the story, your impatience would be so much fretted that you would hang yourself.'

Can we feel that the nouveau roman is the supremely necessary and vital revolution its authors think it to be? Certainly there is no point in reading it if what you expect is to be told something new and penetrating about human motives. Its value lies elsewhere. In the effort to write *en une forme non encore formulée* about the relationship between man and his world, and in such light as it throws into odd corners of this relationship. And more, much more, in the acid sharpness and, at its best, ballet-like skill of the writing. What a relief after the pulpy matter of A. and B., my two lively *bêtes d'aversion.*

At its best, the nouveau roman is an urbane highly intellectual species, demanding infinite precision in its use of language. The reading of *Dans le labyrinthe* gave me moments of the kind of pleasure to be got from listening to a ballade by Chopin. The reiterated images, all strictly visual, touch the same nerve in the mind as the ordered succession of notes, with the same delicacy, though not the same vigour.

Certain brief passages in Nathalie Sarraute's work, moments, vignettes – women, holding bored children by the hand, pausing to stare in shop windows, a child oppressed by the kindly egoism of an adult, a pedant degutting poets – do communicate sharply not only the images themselves but the emotions they mask. They can be compared with passages in *The Notebook of Malte Laurids Brigge*, or with the shorter poems in T. S. Eliot's *Prufrock* volume.

But the work even of Robbe-Grillet, controlled by an acute mind, is attenuated, literary in an anaemic narrowly sophisticated way. The intricacies of his *propre esthétique* are the most important thing he has to give. He has gone a step beyond Henry James's dictum that 'the content and the importance of a work of art are in fine wholly dependent on its *being* one', to deflate content so brutally that what is left exists as a skeletal form, like the brittle veins of a dry leaf. 'The genuine writer has nothing to say. He has only a way of speaking. He must create a world starting from nothing.' Brave words. We expect a miracle. Create your world, we tell him. He creates it. It turns out to be the hallucinatory world of an obsessed man, or almost unbreathable, rarefied to the point where the heart stops.

Sensitive, intelligent, discriminating, civilised – these adjectives can be applied to the nouveau roman with a good conscience and some gratitude. The quality it lacks, the quality that marks the great novelists – using with caution a term which is not another word meaning sensitive, intelligent, civilised – has nothing to do with charm, or the creation of plausible well-constructed plots and characters. The characters of the novels we return to endlessly may be as madly implausible as Charlus or old Karamazov, or as remote from our experience as Heathcliff: what gives them their permanence is the superhuman energy with which they were conceived, the sensual and intellectual depths at which their author lived his knowledge of them.

This is true of Kafka, confined in a world little wider than a valley between mountains of rock. Unable to free himself from the forces crushing him, K. still acts. The cruel and malicious indifference he confronts has a human face and soul. It is an absurd error to make him a forerunner of the nouveau roman, in which man, even when given a physical presence (as he is not in *Jalousie*, where only jealousy has a ghostly existence), is an object in a non-human world.

The conventions of the nouveau roman, the insistence that formal achievement, the divine game of composition, is of the first importance, are not less an orthodoxy than any earlier critical doctrine. Like all orthodoxies, it is made to fit the apostolical hand. It is an impure – should I say imprudent? – use of language. Language, any language, is made up of unnumbered separate structures, words themselves are structures subject to change and deformation. In the very act of shaping a portion of reality they betray it. It is entirely impossible to subdue them to behaving as the neutral vehicle of an emotion, an idea, a state of mind. The more strenuous the writer's effort to convey directly a sensation – the sensation, say, of jealousy – or a fragment of the under-mind's continual dialogue with itself, the less he traps in his verbal net. The substance runs away like a drop of mercury from a broken mirror.

The embarrassing truth is that the novel is *essentially* an impure form, kept alive on a mixed diet, and when purified becomes tuberculous, etiolated, and threatened by the death so often announced. Life at the level on which the classic novelists approached it is full of unassimilable lumps of clay, insoluble contradictions. Intent on the difficulties of his method, the pure novelist is forced to exclude too many of these, and without being able to achieve the concentrated emotional charge of poetry. The writer becomes too important, the novel too elegantly emaciated and bloodless. Too often the perfected form masks the poverty of the matter, the banality of the thought. Carried too far, the process risks death by austerity.

I must say, a more dignified death than that to which most of our novels are sentenced at birth.

In this latest battle of the books I cannot persuade myself to fly into a passion on the side either of the inflexibly traditional novel or of the aggressively new. Those who deride the nouveau roman as arid and pretentious, and those who damn the traditionalist as having no function and no virtue in the epoch of Husserl, Einstein and nuclear physics, are, both of them, more anxious to register themselves as vessels of the one truth, the one correct doctrine, than to engage in a polite discussion. I have an Athenian curiosity about any new thing, and the practitioners of the nouveau roman – architects, mechanics, midwives, camp followers – have given me (except for the last) roughly equal parts of interest and boredom. I understand well enough what they are doing, and why they want to do it. Hence I can afford to be amiable. I think coldly that Robbe-Grillet goes as far as a novelist can go in keeping an unfashionable subjectivity out of his work. To go farther – to go as far as Philippe Sollers (or as Michel Butor in his latest and least accessible text) – lands novelist and reader in an obscurity too deliberate to be better than indulgence in an esoteric word game.

There is no reason why Sollers or any other should not indulge himself. I would not want to deprive him of his pleasure in an intellectual form of suicide as a writer, or his readers, few as they may be, of the pleasure of watching the motions of a subtle mind. That the writers of the *nouveau* nouveau roman – already with us – should interest themselves in linguistic technicalities to the point of self-extinction as novelists is their business. They choose to do it, it amuses them and like-minded readers. Why not? Why not accept it for what it is, a certain attitude to reality, to what is ambiguous and finally obscure in human emotions and conduct, one among other possible and potentially fruitful attitudes, influenced, uncertainly, by modern scientific speculations? That the new novelist's intentions are the antithesis of those of the classic novelist is a childish reason for quarrelling with him.

Frankly, I am often bored by the end result of his intentions. But not to the point of wishing that he did not exist. Indeed I should regret his disappearance. To the eyes of the traditional novelist – Tolstoy, say, or George Eliot, looking at him from the ancient parapets of the novel – he may appear as a barbarian intent on undermining the city. But –

> Some people arrived from the frontiers
> And they said there are no longer any barbarians.
> And now what will become of us without any barbarians?

Formidably learned, even cultivated, these newest barbarians are in their way ascetics, desert Fathers. Their intransigence, even their arrogance, may be prophylactic, a corrective of sorts, even at times a needed emetic. That the difficulty of decoding their novels – or anti-novels – is sometimes ill-rewarded is neither here nor there.

*

What I believe is that we are at the end of an era in the novel, not at the beginning of a new one. Not yet. The experimenters, even the most intelligent, charming, amusing, a Robbe-Grillet, a Christine Brooke-Rose, are a flourish – like the final bars of Rosenkavalier, signed by a pirouette – not a new start.

I am the surer of this when I reflect on the novels of the two greatest and boldest experimenters of our age, infinitely bolder, infinitely more impressive, than any of the others. In *Ulysses* Joyce strained the resources of language to a limit he himself could not overstep without breaking it down and reshaping it to convey a highly subjective and eccentric vision of reality – in the strict sense of eccentric, not in the central current of written language. *Finnegans Wake* is the one major work of fiction which more or less obeys Mallarmé's dictum that *le monde est fait pour aboutir à un beau livre*: to write it he used words to embody a reality intelligible only in relation to the activity of his own mind, not by its reference to the objective world – which includes the minds of other human beings. He is in no sense a surrealist writer: he does not try to dodge past the control of the conscious mind. Never was a more self-conscious writer. He knew, very precisely, what he was about. As in *Ulysses*, but with a colder more besetting will, he watched himself at work, an eccentric genius in the role of an eccentric genius. Using immense intellectual ingenuity to distort the structure of language, dislocating sense and sound, inserting an arbitrary sense (more arbitrary, that is, than the sense millennially agreed) into the gap between them, bending logic to dumbfound logic and sense to mock sense. The very perfection of his method is a measure of its final defeat: what the intricate contortions of his writing expose is a dead body, language broken down into its elements, as in a laboratory, expressive in the last resort of nothing very much. This particular revolt against the pinchbeck and devitalised clichés of a mass society and mass media has never been pushed farther than he pushed it: impossible to imagine anyone cultivating fruitfully his immense Waste Land. No other great novelist has bent his intellect to prepetuate chaos. Like a vast cairn, *Finnegans Wake* marks the end of a road.

Both books, his monument, which seemed to inject energy into the novel by making it free of new country, in fact led it into the splendid but airless museum reserved for works that demand endless explanation (alas, they get it). *Ulysses* is easy enough to read, as its successor is not, and the appalling boredom of stretches of it spring, perhaps, from its relentless piling up of the details of physical existence, as if he had determined knowingly to leave nothing out, to present a *catalogue raisonné*, a realistic novel to end all realism. Which in a sense it does.

You could say that he dismembered language to create from it an aesthetic object without any organic relation to the life either of the solitary individual or of man in society. He was coming near an abandonment of communication, near *felo-de-se* as a writer.

He stopped a long way short of his successor on this road. It is not – or it was not to me – evident in Samuel Beckett's earlier novels that he was any sort of successor to anyone. It now occurs to me that he and Joyce share a mysterious impulse, something in the nature of a rare disease – the disease being as unusual as the writers it attacks. The deepest instinct of a writer's nature is to communicate his experience of life, and to do it through language, itself in the last resort a mystery. How explain the impulse which transforms, at a profound level, the instinct to communicate into the instinct to destroy the lines of communication, to distort language radically, to tear up the roots? Some deep contempt for his fellow-creatures? I don't know.

Beckett has two virtues lacking in Joyce, a superb economy of words and a streak of humour, savage humour, it is true, directed not only against what is neither good nor true, but against the defect we name unhappiness. A humour, a laughter, separated by the thinnest of membranes from a howl of misery and rage, and passing easily from mockery of what is only pretentious to mock what is deformed, weak, or lustful. Does he see any difference in the sexual act as performed by men and dogs? Occasions when he lapses into tenderness are few – at the moment I recall only Krapp's memory of a minute in a punt in sunlight, stretched unmoving across a woman with his face between her breasts and his hand on her.

Joyce understood guilt, but none of his protagonists, not even Stephen in his blackest moods, suffer the sense of ineluctable guilt Beckett's carry about with them at the roots of their being. A Cathar out of his time, Beckett can write (in *Malone*

Dies), 'his semen had never done harm to anyone'. In the context, any Cathar Perfect might have said it. His sense of the irredeemable evil of the created world is absolute and uncompromising: the face the world turns to him is the one it might turn to a child dying of hunger. He has that child in him.

With Schopenhauer he believes that in any life pain is the rule and joy the rare exception, that cruelty is endemic in human beings and the only certainty death. In such a world small pleasures, a green leaf, a child's spontaneous laugh, have no value.

If he believes in God it is a Cathar belief: the God who saves is absent in *Waiting for Godot*; the evil creator of our world is at best indifferent, at worst wantonly cruel – Sam and Watt are agreed that they come closest to God when they engage in an act of revolting cruelty. And, if he cannot have the absent God, there is nothing else he wants – 'All that is not God is dung', even the beauty of the world.

Wastes of scatology and violent obscenity prefigure a life in which man is lost, a damned soul, tormented by his sense of the absurdity and utter senselessness of existence, absolutely alone, unable to make any contact with others, at the mercy of such instincts as he has not killed in himself. No single physical or intellectual possibility offered to him is worth the trouble of engaging in it.

The earlier novels have echoes of Sterne, and passages of delicacy, acuteness of perception, of sight and sound, simple human emotions, even speculations. With each successive book these get fewer, until we reach *le murmure dans la boue* to which in his all but autistic imagination life is reduced. The search for a meaning in *Ping* (1967) might amuse, endlessly and vainly, a mind able to take pleasure in the chaotic repetition of phrases and words. Are they, perhaps, fragments of consciousness drifting through the brain of a dying man? Is this writing, like Stockhausen's music, a new mode of notation it is impossible to respond to except by rejecting every expectation a lifetime of listening and reading has rooted in ear and mind? I don't know. What I do know, what I am sure of, is that in this stage of his writing, Beckett is turning literature against itself. His retreat from the word (the phrase is George Steiner's) reduces language to an end game. Beyond it, nothing. A void. Silence.

Like two Easter Island statues, man-made monuments unfriendly to man, Joyce and Beckett stand on the furthermost frontier of the classic novel, each in his way a reminder that the novel as an aesthetic experience is not an absolute, not complete. To suppose that it is recalls the claim of the mediaeval alchemists to be seeking or discovering a final truth and wisdom. The notion of art as an autonomous state transcending both artist and audience is as magnificent an illusion. Illusions have their uses, they allow us to live, each in our desert cell, as if it were the garden of Epicurus, but let them, in some cold lucid corner of the mind, be recognised as illusion, without regret, without any sense of defeat. Men, including writers, are what they are, 'contaminated', to borrow Robbe-Grillet's phrase for a purpose he would consider illegitimate, by the human instinct to give meaning and coherence to disintegration itself.

6. The retreat from the pleasure principle

In the millennial debate between critics persuaded that imaginative literature is created to please and those who think it should serve manners or morals, the hedonists had the best of it. The death of Hector, the lamentations of the Trojan women, the cruelties of the sagas, the agony of Lear, were meant to give pleasure by the manner of their telling, by what it reveals of the human spirit. Their writers' purpose was not to civilise the tribe – nor indeed have they had very much success in that field – but to enrich the senses and engage the mind. In the long history of criticism, few of the great critics considered that it could or should be otherwise. Neither did the writers. Even a writer whose aim was to exhort and purify knew or feared that he must first or also please.

We have changed all that.

That voguish American writer, Miss Susan Sontag, notes the change, but not, I think, correctly. 'Another way of characterising the present cultural situation, in its most creative aspects, would be to speak of a new attitude towards pleasure. In one sense, the new art and the new sensibility take a rather dim view of pleasure . . . If hedonism means sustaining the old ways in which we have found pleasure in art (the old sensory and psychic modalities) then the new art is anti-hedonistic. Having one's sensorium challenged or stretched hurts. The new serious music hurts one's ears, the new films and the few interesting new prose works do not go down easily . . . But the purpose of art is, always, ultimately, to give pleasure – though our

77

sensibilities may take time to catch up with the forms of pleasure that art in a given time may offer.'

To think only of literature, nothing in the contemporary field stretches the whole range of our senses as they are stretched by *Medea* or the *Duchess of Malfi* or *The Possessed*. Were great novels ever intended to go down easily? Did they? *Middlemarch*? *War and Peace*? *A la recherche du temps perdu*? *Der Mann ohne Eigenschaften*? What is more, her assertion that the purpose of art is always, ultimately, to give pleasure fails to take account of an obvious change in the attitude of some modern novelists. Call it a retreat from the pleasure principle. That sounds reassuringly Freudian – but is not at once enlightening.

What is happening is the rise to the surface of a new cold current in the novel. It is difficult to say at what point it emerged. At what moment in the evolution of the novel did the impulse to tell the awful truth about the horror and absurdity of life, to strip human life of meaning and the human being of dignity, take precedence in the minds of some writers over the older impulse to present as steadily observed a vision of reality as possible, with no more intention *to show life up* – as senseless and ugly – than Homer when he described a young man's death at Achilles' pitiless hands – *So, friend, you die also* . . .?

No absolute reason why a writer should not, if he is so moved, use his talents to instruct, or denounce, or reduce man to his status as a poor forked radish. *Nous avons tous notre gibier.* The point at issue is the change in sensibility and purpose.

Perhaps it started effectively with the Goncourts, with their solemn rather naïve belief that their born task as writers was to shock out of his complacency the bourgeois philistine whose tastes and social assumptions they despised. 'Aujourd'hui que le Roman . . . commence à être la grande forme sérieuse, passionnée, vivante, de l'étude littéraire et l'enquête social . . .

[et] s'est imposé les études et les devoirs de la science . . .'
Which being interpreted meant something less than it said.

The first great realists of the nineteenth century, including
Stendhal, extending the boundaries of fiction to take in
political, social, and economic developments, had not made a
manifesto of it. Nor were the Goncourts – in this unlike Zola –
interested in these developments for their own sake; they were
interested primarily in tearing the rags off the putrefying body
of bourgeois society and its commercial ethos, and the pleasure
they chiefly sought was the pleasure it gave them to express
themselves and their distaste and curiosity by telling the unpleasant or repulsive truth. Not only must the novel be truth-
ful, but if the truth is ugly so much the more meritorious the
novelist's effort.

I am being much less than just to the Goncourts. They
would find crudely unaesthetic those living novelists who
exploit the confusion and indignities of a society in which not
only all is permitted, but abuse of the self and of others obligatory. As indeed would the founder of the abbey of Thélème,
intended for 'men that are free, well-born, well-bred, and con-
versant in honest companies.' He would hold his nose at the
stench rising from some well-praised modern novels, a very
curious stench, compounded of hostility not merely to a
condemned society but to such civilisation as exists, delight in
mocking the humble necessary virtues of gentleness and self-
sacrifice, and an impulse, conscious or involuntary, to show up
human nature in its more brutal, more addle-pated forms. Not
to speak of their barbarous way with language, a habit at
the opposite pole from Rabelais' pleasure in teaching it new
steps.

Ankle deep in this new current, we are a long way from the
idea of pleasure as a Good, in life or literature. Some simplicity
has been lost. The classic Greeks knew everything about ugli-
ness and cruelty, but they kept their heads, their capacity for

reverence and wonder, their capacity for delight. So did most writers of every century until the last. No doubt the decline was inevitable. The intellect devours its children.

Is it possible that the instinct involved really is that dark instinct Freud thought he had detected? The turning of the face away from life towards extinction. A refusal to look for pleasure in literature wherever it used to be found, wherever the free mind could discover gaiety, sensual warmth, dignity in the madness of Quixote, light in Oedipus' eyeless sockets, a kernel of joy in defeat. What is most noticeable about the description of acts of cruelty so common in novels now is the minute laboured detail, like the fingers of a child carefully vivisecting an insect.

A fissure has opened in the imagination: the aggressive instinct we honour in war and make secret use of in civic torture is showing its face in places where it used to be cold-shouldered, in films, plays, novels, and receiving the applause of lettered critics.

I have a shrewd notion that when Miss Sontag spoke of 'the few interesting new prose writers', she was thinking of Mr William Burroughs, whose borborygmus style has the same effect on me as thinking about Grenoble had on Stendhal, *comme le souvenir d'une abominable indigestion*. Has she not somewhere described him as 'the most serious, urgent, and original voice in American letters to be heard for many years'?

(Original? Well, perhaps, yes, in the sense of my Yorkshire childhood, when it was said by indulgent adults of a child not naturally defective, but deliberately behaving like a clown, 'Eeh, he's an original.')

*

The eruption into common daylight of more or less literate pornographic fiction is the only wholly new direction taken since the second war: it has received nearly as much critical attention and respect as electronic music and M. Marcel Duchamp's urinal.

Only its sudden rise to the surface is new; bawdy is as old as writing, and no doubt as old as story-telling. To class it, obsessed as it is with one form of pleasure, as a retreat from the pleasure principle is not perverse. Simply, it is irrational to try to make the same term cover the pleasure given by Stendhal and that given by a meticulous description of coitus and sodomy. Irrational? Well, of course. Only reflect that the pleasures to be expected from literature have always included intellectual delight, and that the intellect, which plays as eagerly with passions as with ideas, cannot find a great deal to amuse it in a novel concerned to repeat, in a necessarily limited and repetitive vocabulary, variants of the same familiar act, the same set of reflexes. The two pleasures are so monstrously unlike that to confound them under one head is absurd and slovenly.

Reading contemporary criticism, you might suppose that the terms *erotic novel* and *pornography* are interchangeable. That they are used as though they were is part of the slovenliness.

Hunger, ambition, parenthood, the controlled ferocities of the artist and the scientist, can at any moment, in any individual, elbow the sexual impulse aside; none of them equals it in complexity and range of energy. It is the underlying note of existence, an intricate web of pleasure and anguish spread through life. It interferes with these other powerful impulses at all levels: the sexual aspect of ambition or intellectual research is detached from the need itself but not from its procreative energy. It penetrates literature on all levels. An ignorant child below the age of puberty can eroticise a story of the Indian Mutiny by transferring sensations of excitement to organs he does know the use of. The 'infernal world' invented and described in so many thousands of lines of microscopic writing by the young Brontës was fed from deeply erotic sources.

Calling up the image of the Duke of Zamorna leaning against an obelisk, Charlotte almost fainted – 'I was quite gone . . . I felt myself breathing quick and short.' Many imaginative children indulge in such day-dreams, dubiously innocent, mental games played on a level some distance below the cross-roads turning off in later life towards pornography or genuine erotic art.

To celebrate sensual and sexual love, show it as the subtlest form of kindness between bodies, show it blazing, absorbing, possibly destroying – *Vénus toute entière à sa proie attachée* – an involvement of the whole nervous system, an ecstasy not only of the sexual parts, but of every other organ, including the brain, stretches the novelist's inventive subtlety and force, his capacity for experience and its re-creation in words, to their limit. Should he be moved to portray physical details, the degree of his success is measurable by his readers' sense of their point and moment as part of the bodily and spiritual disturbance touched off by the erotic impulse, going far beyond the act.

The use in erotic literature of sexual terms and gestures is neither here nor there. The intensely erotic writing of the early Mauriac, of Proust, Thomas Mann, Montherlant, Malraux, John Cowper Powys, has no need of either. Nor, on the other hand, is their use what makes a novel a pornographic work. The detailed descriptions of the sexual act in *Les deux étendards*, by that unhappy novelist, now after his escape from execution as a collaborator, living obscurely in Paris, Lucien Rebatet, are splendidly, at times savagely erotic; they are not pornographic, since at every moment the reader is aware of other emotions and sensations than the narrowly sexual. The supplest and most complex sympathies of the imagination are involved.

Literature is concerned to explore and illumine the infinite possibilities of the whole man. Your simple-minded professional pornographer, playing over his few notes on the genital organ, is anything you like to call him, a humble worker for a pittance, an exciter of solitary lusts, a wretch, a benefactor of the lonely, anything but a writer of erotic novels. The mass-produced pornography which used to be secluded in small seedy shops had, has, only one aim: to excite its readers sexually. Like the writing of a party hack or a professional advertiser, it is committed writing, intended to stimulate or coerce its readers to an action. It has a strictly non-literary end in view. Boring to the adult mind, exciting to the adolescent or sexually immature, pornography of this plain lewd sort probably does neither harm nor good to its users.

Literary pornography also intends to excite, but it is a much odder quirk of the mind. It is an ill-charted continent, running away at one pole to sadism (not invariably as laboured and piteously boring as the Marquis de Sade's *One Hundred and Twenty Days of Sodom*), and at the opposite pole to a crop of novels which flirt genteelly with indecency, and in which the characters 'have sex' – surely the most nauseatingly coy phrase ever invented? – between bouts of gossipy foreign travel or flaccid mysticism or talk of Baudelaire and Catullus.

The pornography of a serious writer, a Swinburne, a Verlaine, an Apollinaire, an Aragon (if so be he wrote *Le con d'Irène*, which he vigorously denies) will bear the thumb-mark of its author. Why a genuinely imaginative writer is moved to write a pornographic novel is a mildly interesting speculation. A regressive defiance, the impulse of an adolescent to shock, to amuse himself by shocking? A species of verbal voyeurism, the revival of the sensations roused in an inquisitive child or an impotent or sexually deprived man or woman by watching a coupling? A semi-adult form of the pleasure a child takes in fantasies confusedly connected with the orifices and organs of his own body? The impulse at a more nearly adult level to show what splendidly fearless animals we are, or would be if we had the courage of our needs? But the sex even in serious pornography has less singularity than the mating of squirrels. By cutting the sexual act out of the complex web of human relationships, to expose it in the form of a naïve recital of bodily gestures and sensations, its authors make everything much too easy for themselves. Nothing, but nothing, is so easy to describe as physical postures. What Romeo may have done with the parts of his body, or what he said in the act, his creator did not think worth recording. Since what he wanted was to give a sense of overwhelming erotic delight, its intensity would have been lowered and dulled by insisting on attention to the animal gestures.

Pornography is essentially reductive, an exercise in the nothing-but mode, a depersonalising of the human beings involved, a showing-up of human lust as nothing but an affair of the genitals. Reduced to a conjunction of bodies, a display of faintly ridiculous sexual athletics, it becomes tedious or as almost inconceivably silly as the masturbating housemaid in *An American Dream*, noisy misbirth of an immensely talented writer and rude moralist. It needs an effort to take the incontinent authors of these things seriously, not to dismiss them as what in my barbarous northern childhood we spoke of as 'fond apes'.

Or is it possible that the stressing, by writers lacking neither intelligence nor moral energy, of the details of coitus, crudely, clumsily, sometimes with a clear trace of disgust, is a form of exhibitionism, a nervous tic rather than a creative impulse of a writer in control of his energies? A sort of self-voyeurism – as in persons who enjoy making love in front of a looking-glass? Or in effect confessional, as on a psychoanalyst's couch, of aberrations, autoerotic fantasies, or normal impulses which do not get an airing in everyday intelligent conversation?

*

If the solemn portrayal, by formally adult writers, of two

persons engaged in sexual activity makes me yawn or starts in me that jeering ironic Yorkshire laughter I dislike and try to silence in myself, I don't yawn and cannot laugh at sadistic pornography, at its account of sexual torture, flagellation, onanism, enforced bestiality. I think coolly that its authors need the attention of a psychiatrist or should be encouraged to write and tear up, that its publishers are sordid fellows who would sell their grandmothers to make soup, and that critics who praise it on whatever grounds – verbal skill, the virtues of free speech, what you will – are either charlatans or pedantic followers of any new fashion.

All pornography is to a degree sadistic – inevitably. Not only is there an element of aggression in all physical attraction, but the insistence that there is nothing more in sexual passion than the pursuit of an orgasm (blessed word) strips the characters of their humanity, and sex itself of that friendship between bodies which, we are told, the gods themselves envy us. The least bearable quality of such novels as *The Naked Lunch* and *An American Dream* – apart from the appalling monotony of the minutiae of fornication and sodomy and the rest of it – is the total absence of common gentleness and humility. Silliness, derision, hate, in plenty, and barely a grain of human warmth. For all I know to the contrary, their authors are admirable persons, who would not hang a mouse. And for all I remind myself that there is no fathoming the cess-pool of human cruelty, I don't at all clearly understand why they are moved not to understand but to exploit it. Why, in short, they are moved to join in the progressive dehumanising of areas of human sensibility. There must be some intellectual and instinctual kinship between the unhappy unshriven persons who seek gratification in inflicting pain (or suffering it) and writers who enjoy writing about it – no serious writer writes what he does not enjoy writing. It eludes me.

Tentatively, I put forward two clues. From so much of this

seriously-intended pornography there rises, even when it is lewdly or boisterously comic, the acrid smell, unmistakable, of self-dislike. It is very noticeable in William Burroughs's work, accepted by reputable critics and some of his fellow-writers as 'a great novelist'. His intention runs far past the obligatory obscenity of actions and language, to turn against and castrate the human instincts themselves. I am genuinely puzzled by the eagerness of any intelligent man or woman to accept as erotic literature the efforts of a writer so revolted by his physical humanity that he labours to make it dull and disgusting to readers. They would be more intelligently employed following to its source the inverted prudery and self-hatred, the underlying distaste for sexual energy and delight. Why he hates himself is no concern of mine. He is rebelling, yes. It is possible to guess against what. But for what? If his intention was to cut off at their source the sensual springs of literature, could he have gone about it more ingeniously than in *The Naked Lunch*? Or marked more clearly the point at which an attack on convention, on a society bullied by the machine (including the bureaucratic machine) – an attack in subtler hands life-giving and gay – becomes an attack on our self-respect and decent self-love? The roots joining a literature of self-hatred and self-contempt to the concentration camp world run underground. But they run.

It is agreed, today, that a sense of guilt is a moral flaw, and should be got rid of in themselves by the enlightened. But the smell of guilt is as strong in sadistic pornography as the other smell. Is it conceivable that its begetters, below the level on which they are consciously working, are still afflicted with the notion of sexual pleasure as sinful, to be punished? For the sexual sadist, the other person is degraded to seem an object, a receptacle for the discharge of his energies and fantasies. The sacrificial victim he humiliates and torments may be expiating in his place *his* sin, the unforgivable sin of exercising power at the expense of a fellow-creature. It may be that in one and the same act he satisfies his mania to possess absolutely and punishes himself for it.

Inevitably, the flood of literary pornography loosed on us is dulling our reactions of surprise or shock. Its writers are forced to raise the ante, to provide stronger and stronger stimulants. Or try to provide them, since both the manner, the naming of parts and the few inexpressive four-letter words, and the matter, are narrowly limited. The last novel in this kind I read and read seriously, in honest enquiry – and my goodness it is the last, my endurance of boredom and mental nausea is also limited – piles up everything, torture, sodomy, paederasty, a syphilitic poet too poor to afford paper and writing his great poem in charcoal on pages of the *Chicago Tribune*, the details of a peculiarly horrible abortion, homosexuals bawling about their miseries, the odd incest. Its compiler, James Purdy, described by one of the most intelligent of living critics as 'a writer of fantastic talent', not only outdoes every previous labourer in the field known to me, but – surely? – has reached a frontier beyond which

> Thy hand, great Anarch! lets the curtain fall
> And Universal Dulness buries all.

It falls on a soldier, tortured, brutally raped, tied to a tree and beaten, finished off at last by a long iron weapon 'of monstrous design'. All very phallic and symbolic, a crude symbolism – '. . . the captain without a word began his work, pushing like flame with the instrument into Daniel's groin upward and over, and then when its work was nearing completion he put his face to Daniel's and pressing said something, in bloody accolade, that not even Daniel heard.'

Not only does this rhetoric start up ludicrous echoes of the ejaculations in horror comics, but the effect – of terror and agony – is infinitely feebler than that of a comparable scene in

La condition humaine, related with a cold intensity and calm that sear to the bone.

The significant point is that – *pace* the eminent critic – this elaborate effort to outshock the field, by a reputed and far from unintelligent novelist, over-written as it is, has the regressive quality common to all pornographic fiction, commonplace trash or serious. Its characters are blown out like carnival figures, they weep abundantly, they are continually turning pale, they rave about their love in all the clichés of lush romance, or cannot bring themselves to tell it to the loved one. What was surely designed to express the physical brutality of a brutal society exposes little except the hollowness of sentimental fiction standing on its head.

Could it, given the author's talent, have turned out otherwise? I believe not.

The language, too, lapses from rhetoric into silliness – 'Biting his lips like a traitor, he said . . .' Do you know, you, how to make a difference when you bite your lips like a traitor and when you are biting them in annoyance or from habit?

*

Why is it, do you suppose, that the pornographic novel has so almost suddenly broken cover to become a critical event?

An intelligent novelist does not write, does not handle language, in a literary vacuum, he stands in an only partly self-dictated relation to society, and writes what in some degree is a response to it, a criticism of, a judgement on it. A new attitude to society, a new social myth, must be taking shape behind the dust of argument.

Every myth is janus-faced. It is both an effort to grasp mentally and emotionally what is felt as an obscure and dangerous force in nature and an impulse to mock it. Death is seen as eloquent, just and mighty, and as comic, the last absurd slip on a banana-skin. Sexual passion is an 'object strange and high . . . begotten by despair Upon impossibility,' or an affair of bodily needs and postures little less ludicrous than the sexual antics of penguins. Bawdy amusement and wonder, even awe, are twisted together at the roots of the structure of human sexuality. What is of new interest in the pornographic novel is its emergence at this moment as a recognised literary form, or a public menace – depending on your sensibility.

Its wholehearted admirers see it as a great gesture of moral and intellectual liberation: the mind has been set free to explore unhindered an area of sensual experience, vitally, overwhelmingly important, hitherto repressed and degraded by taboos and hypocrisies. With a perhaps less disinterested enthusiasm, its publishers say as much. The eloquence of a pioneer in the business of making pornographic fiction accessible to a hungry multitude, Mr Maurice Girodias, though pitched a little high, is canonical. 'But in a maturing society the rights of the individual gradually regain precedence. The phenomenon is particularly remarkable in England today, probably because Victorian repression was so intolerably priggish. The smouldering fire has suddenly erupted into a beautiful explosion, shattering all the windows of the Establishment. Fire has issued forth from the loins of one Mellors, from Molly Bloom's libido; fire has erupted from Henry Miller's mammoth groin, from William Burroughs' spastic mannikins. This is war, this is revolution.' (*Encounter*: February 1966)

This is fine whipping-in talk. And do not be too much put out by erupting groins: enthusiasm plays the deuce with metaphors.

The germ of sense in the loose rhetoric is that Victorian prudery and fears – fear of losing self-control and fear of losing control of women and other possessions – did lay a dead hand on attempts to write freely and candidly about sexual passion in all the forms it takes. The violence of the vengeful reaction is thus in part a legacy from a long period of bigotry, patriarchal restraint, compulsory swaddling clothes. It is a great many other things: the pleasure of frightening the sober citizen with the spectre of his own repressed violence; the still more exhilarating pleasure of flaunting your rejection of a bourgeoisie whose standards, manners, and conformism you despise. And a remote, a caricatural, reflection of Rimbaud's image of himself as a deranged outlaw. Perhaps a society gets the pornographers it deserves.

Myself born a rebel against authority, I prefer any naïve declaration of rights to the vulgar farce of commending pornography as sexual hygiene, a form of therapy. Possibly it is, but, merciful heavens, does anyone genuinely expect a sanitary service to give birth to a literary renaissance? Nor has it done so. With a very few exceptions, the energies freed by the eruption have issued in novels, plays, films, of minimal interest. It may be true that when creative energy is allowed to run away in an obsession with sexual details, it loses heat. No doubt, the novelist writes with his loins and groin as well as with his brain, nerves, and the fluid in his veins, but perhaps they should be controlled?

It may seem a little absurd to see the writers of the newest pornographic fiction as part of the confused revolt against a society in which machines in the service of the Great Interests are turning men into cogs. But what is absurd is not, not necessarily, untrue. The pressures of a triumphant technocracy – ever-increasing mechanisation and automation not simply of industry but of all aspects of daily living, the ever-increasing intrusion of bureaucratic controls into our private lives and freedom of movement – affect us doubly, in body and spirit. Over against the powerful and immensely intricate machinery of finance, modern politics, electronic media, driving society towards totalitarianism of one or another or no colour, in nearly irresponsible reaction to it, sprawls the anarchic world – anarchic even when harnessed to commerce – of the pop groups and their screaming adolescent audiences, of quick-witted panders who draw their profit from promoting a collapse into mindlessness, of Carnaby Street in all its incarnations, of the poor self-defeated victims of LSD, of cynical knowingness about human relationships. It is not only the very young, not only the lewd, who cannot pass a monument of the past without lifting a leg against it.

The eruption from their fiery loins may be a revolt on the easiest imaginative level, but it is not inconceivable – since writers write in the hope of being read – that its communicants see it also, over and above their mission to bring light to them that sit in darkness and the shadow of conventional pieties, as a chance of making themselves heard above the roar of a thousand million television sets.

Now that so many of the once living nerves between the individual and society are atrophied, and with the virtual disappearance of the old comforting fraternal rituals, the old communions, religious and social, almost the last self-evident link the single human being can forge between himself and what is not himself is through his sex. It is the one wholly inalienable personal experience. Hence the excessive attention paid to it at every turn now, down to the debased art of the advertiser. Hence, too, the latent hostility, the almost hatred, libertines of either sex feel for their collaborators, born of disappointment in the meagre emotional return for so much desperate expense of energy.

The mocking paradox is that pornographic fiction is itself part of the alienated world of abstractions and mechanical living. Its frenzied concern with the technique of achieving sexual satisfaction, heterosexual, homosexual, or sadistic, has too narrow an area to move about in, the situations and responses soon begin to seem computerised. Even in cunning hands the subject becomes a bore, like the ghastly boredom of listening to a man (or woman) relating his sexual triumphs and miseries, with always the moment when the most attractive suddenly turns under one's eye into a performing animal.

Poor Lawrence, who supposed that the sexual scenes in *Lady Chatterley's Lover* were a holy work, a high mass of human passion and physical love, would have been chilled by the latter-day celebrants of the orgasm. It is all to the good that what he called 'the mind's terror of the body' should be exorcised. The more difficult question is how, while liberating the mind, to civilise the body.

Sex, the dedicated pornographer insists – as if we didn't know – permeates life. When he treats it in fiction it permeates only two anatomies. That is why his boldest scenes are often coldly bathetic. They leave out the essential. They ask us to accept repetitions of familiar bodily movements in two anonymous bodies – very much as in those American faculty wives who demonstrated onanism before the researchers' cameras – in place of the wholeness of personal experience.

In the end it is not a question of good or bad, precise or slovenly writing. The lucid and supple prose John Updike has taught himself to use, an instrument capable, you would suppose, of any miracle of communication, fails to communicate anything more than an appalling boredom when in his latest novel he undertakes to give a cannily frank and lively account of the sexual *chasse-croisé* of ten married couples. Beyond a point fixed by the reader's goodwill towards an immensely talented writer, the book becomes strictly unreadable – unless by persons whose curiosity Mr Updike may or may not have wanted to gratify. Even descriptive passages which have nothing to do with the characters' coital doings and dialogue take on by a sort of verbal osmosis the aspect of an embalmed body, beautiful and lifeless.

In the sensual experience of adult human beings, what is of

compelling interest is never the movements of bodies but the movements of soul, the complex fluctuating motives that dictate our behaviour against our knowledge and will. Stendhal's agony over a woman he never possessed is charged with erotic sensibility and potency to a degree that makes a fumbling schoolboy of the windy author of *The Naked Lunch*.

*

Talk of censorship rouses the most farcical passions in persons otherwise more or less rational. There is little to choose in self-righteousness and irrationality between the outraged moralist and the dogmatic liberal. Because he is fighting a losing battle the first is possibly less of a bore, but it is a near thing. The second's blind insistence that there are no evil human beings, if they behave evilly they are sick, and his equally blind refusal to sanction any check on any form of expression, however senselessly destructive or squalid, makes a dialogue with him difficult: he is in the pulpit, his surplice on, before you can say the Marquis de Sade.

The 'Moors' trial, only too naturally, injected acrimony into an argument that was already more emotional than reasoned. Two sane persons, a man and a young woman, before they killed a little girl carried out on her the sexual tortures prescribed by Sade, and recorded on tape her agonised appeals for mercy. On the man's bookshelves were Sade's novels and other sadistically pornographic works; it could not be and was not denied that he had used them as manuals of conduct.

Two things seem fairly clear. A human being who is cruel by nature – crueller, that is, than at moments or in thought, all humans are – will find ways to make others suffer though he never reads a line of a sadistic book. Or even if he reads only the classics: a love of Goethe never deterred a Nazi official from operating the gas chambers. That is one thing. The other: it is sheer humbug – or sheer pedantry or a lie – to say or think

93

that a sadistic novel has no effect on its readers. An honest man cannot say that he was never, if only when he was young, profoundly disturbed and influenced by some book he read. Disturbed for good or ill, but disturbed, his life and thinking changed. We do not read only with our aesthetic awareness; our whole nervous system is involved, to a greater or lesser degree.

It is conceivable, it is arguably likely, that to read about tortures and acts of sexual degradation will, at the least, reinforce in a reader inclined to cruelty a tendency which might otherwise have been repressed or remained latent. Every reader of *L'histoire d'O* or of Sade's *Justine* does not take to flagellation or torturing. But what might be their effect on a mind balanced on an edge between cerebral lechery or sadism and active experiment?

The argument - I have used it myself - that the sources of human cruelty do not need books to make them overflow is sound. But no one – except a man surer of his knowledge of human nature than anybody has a right to be – can assert that the 'Moors' sadists would have done what they did without having read a line of sadistic pornography. It is possible. *It is not certain.* Those people, the liberal-minded critics or only the publishers of sadistic novels, who are perfectly sure that the censorship of pornography is unnecessary or unhygienic or an intellectual or aesthetic outrage, may be right. But would it not become them, as normally fallible men and women, to think, with less arrogance, that they just possibly might be mistaken? The theory that repression of natural tendencies is always a bad thing – a theory which runs all the way from sparing children the annoyance of being house-trained to leaving the field wide open to Mr Girodias's undiscriminating labours in the cause of total freedom and erupting groins – may have gone too far? Have been too blindly accepted?

It is open to anyone to condemn censorship. The arguments

for not condemning it are rational and cogent. What is irrational, unjustifiable, is to say: The multiplication of these books, and the ease with which they can be got, will not deprave the imagination, will certainly not encourage readers possibly already corrupted, possibly not, to imitate the forms of sexual gratification described for them in exact detail.

To reject censorship after studying the risks involved is very well. To reject it *ex cathedra*, in the tones of Calvin pronouncing a dogma, eyes and mind closed to the possible consequences, the even marginally possible, is to make things too comfortable for oneself.

I have never been able to make up my mind about the censorship of pornography. Or, rather, I make it up one day and unmake it the next. I know the arguments against it rather well. I have used them. I have said: Express yourself as freely as you want, describe exactly how you behave sexually, or would like to – neither I nor anyone is forced to listen. Repression is bad for the soul even when it makes social life pleasanter. The furtive inhibitions of prudes are as nauseating as they always were, heaven forbid that they should ever again be in a position to dictate what we may or may not write or read. The censorship of pornographic literature – or of mass-produced trash – creates more evils than it prevents.

And the rest of it and the rest of it. I am a dogmatic liberal in my hours.

There are other arguments. No one, or no civilised person, wants to see writers hounded by the self-righteous, the hypocritical, the frightened, as Baudelaire, as Flaubert, as Lawrence, were hounded. Rather than let that happen again, should we not accept the risks we run in publishing sadistic literature *à gogo*? What magistrate, what twelve persons, can be trusted to detect that *Lady Chatterley's Lover* is a passionately serious attempt, by a great writer, to describe the act of sex in words as scrupulously honest, as respectful of the complex emotions involved, as possible? (That the attempt is marred by grue-some sentimentality is neither here nor there: the intention was humane.)

Think, too, with smiling pity – since most great enterprises have their farcical side – of the dilemma forced on the literary don, the well-meaning critic, asked to stand up in the witness box and swear that novels of infinitely less worth are to be compared with Dickens or some other classic, because failure to testify in uncompromising terms may mean that the work in question, boring and bad as it is, will be banned.

The ethics of such well-intentioned perjury interest me. Do we praise it as undertaken in defence of literature, because it is better to let a thousand worthless or atrocious books through the net rather than risk strangling a work of genius, or because the witness disapproves so passionately of the practice of banning books that he will swear any nonsense to snatch a victim from burning? Or because censorship is degrading in itself, and if the only way to express abhorrence of it is to praise clumsy or preposterously silly or brutal novels, more's the pity?

It is sad to see honest men morally forced to lie. Minor casualties of Mr Girodias's 'great revolution'. I can think of only one thing that in the circumstances would be even sadder. Suppose that intelligent cultivated persons genuinely believe certain novels and plays to be penetrating social criticism, moving, life-giving.

That really would be something for tears.

And again: not only is a banned book, a prosecution, and the spectacle of writer and publisher fighting for the life of their child in a cloud of witness swearing their tongues off the finest of advertisements, but to all of us, and more acutely to the immature, what is forbidden will always seem worth looking into. Its defenders agree that the quality of much of what they call sex fiction is low, and blame the pent-up pressure released. In time, they argue, writers and readers will become used to their freedom and more discriminating. It is a romantic notion, but arguable. No sane person wants to forbid for the sake of forbidding. Balancing one thing against another, it may well seem that to let pornographic fiction run free will improve its quality, like the eggs of free-range hens, and let it find its own level in the market.

That this last could happen is supported by the Danish experiment. In June 1967 Denmark abolished all prohibitions against written pornography. The sales dropped at once. Six months before the ban was lifted, a new illegal pornographic book sold anything from 20,000 to 25,000 copies. Today only half that number are printed and of these a large percentage is returned unsold from the news-stands and kiosks.

And yet, and yet . . . I am not sure. The advocates of total freedom are sure they are right, the would-be censors are sure. I find it impossible to feel so sure that novels filled with accounts of tortures, beatings, sexual cruelties and humiliations of every sort, are fit for anything but burning. And as impossible to be better than uneasy about bureaucratic censorship. Who willingly trusts a bureaucrat?

Sadistic literature is not only inhumane. It is anti-human. I can at times believe that the writing of a sadistically pornographic novel is itself a sadistic act, the equivalent in literature of the scientific creation of atrociously cruel devices for killing. Neither novelist nor scientist may recognise in himself his deepest, least avowable motive. Each may see himself engaged in boldly intelligent labours, justifying the inalienable right of intellect and imagination to explore any new territory, push to its limit any creative curiosity, and be encouraged in his (unconscious) arrogance by the admiration of his fellows.

There is no dodging the truth that cruelty, from its meanest to its most revolting aspects, is a rooted human trait. It shows itself everywhere: in the respectable guise of a scientist inventing the napalm bomb, in the civil servant planning the use of gas-ovens to get rid of unwanted fellow-creatures. In the judicial tortures carried out in prisons and on the bodies of enemies, and in the sexual cruelty faithfully depicted by a talented writer or put into practice by two persons who slowly did a child to death.

Does it then follow that sadism is as legitimate a subject for the novelist as any other human habit – courage, self-sacrifice, generosity? Is it not better – since no one is compelled to read what makes him vomit – to let the pus discharge itself?

I feel every sort of doubt. To write *in this way* about atrocious acts, as if photographing them, is to exploit them for their sickening effect. Understandable in a man with designs on our pocket. Unforgivable self-indulgence on the part of a writer.

Today the doctrine consecrating total freedom of expression is used on us as a bludgeon (like so many excellent doctrines). Compromise, concede a point, they say, and we shall be back in the nineteenth century, cowering before the philistines, or driven underground by a police censor. The argument is completely irrational, which makes it harder to question. It implies that the only advance of which we are capable is an uncontrolled putsch. This is as odd and boring an idea as that there is some meaningful connection between freedom of expression and the impulse to expose the working of our bodily organs and orifices, the everyday details of copulation, menstruation, excretion, in the greatest possible detail. No doubt there is a connection, but so trivial.

Is it really beyond our wits to devise some form of censorship which would trap only the crudely sadistic? Perhaps a publishers' council could judge when a member of their profession is overstepping a line drawn, not between pornography and erotic literature, not between good and bad writing, but between two sorts of pornography. Not everybody, and not I, would wish to deprive Mr Girodias of the pleasure he has said he feels in having published a novel in which a

countess is serviced by a stallion. Reading such highly implausible nonsense probably does no great harm, though it may
give children in the throes of puberty bad dreams. Sadistic
pornography is acutely another matter. If there is no more than
a chance in a hundred thousand that one child, one, may be
tortured in ways suggested by the reading of sadistic fiction,
that surely is enough to make its publication an error to be committed as seldom as possible?

Censorship by a government official is repugnant. Is it naïve
to think that we might be able to rely on the evolution of a
habit of moral responsibility among publishers? Even among
writers?

*

All my life before the last twenty years I believed with passion
that the enquiring mind and imagination are sacrosanct, that a
scientist has the right and duty to cultivate every area of knowledge, that all that can be known should be. In literature, this
scientific doctrine of the sacred right of the mind to go anywhere, open any door, let out on us any terror, is paralleled by
the artistic doctrine that all forms of experience are worth
exploring. All without exception.

With the best will in the world to be amiable and catholic, I
find this inexcusably sentimental.

Since Hiroshima I have allowed myself to wonder whether
scientists are any more to be trusted with total freedom of
action than the rest of us. In the same spirit I am no longer
certain that all conceivable subjects are worth a serious writer's
energy and time. (What I mean by serious is the exact opposite
of solemn. In a sense, comedy is more serious than tragedy,
which ends in final defeat or the peace of death, where comedy
changes the living. Or it should and can. In good light hands
bawdy is gay, and the laughter it provokes a gift from some
earthy god.)

Some subjects may simply have become unusable by a self-respecting writer. The theme of seduction, for instance. When Laclos wrote *Les liaisons dangereuses* the seduction of a well-brought-up virgin was a serious affair, might end in appalling misery. The complacent hobbledehoy of Mr Amis's *Take a Girl Like You*, who at the end of the book succeeds in raping the young woman he has been pursuing, runs no risks, and rouses in us no emotion beyond mild contempt for his methods. Now that seduction is of no social or moral importance, it has perhaps become impossible for a novelist to find in it any incitement to handle the situation in depth. Or could a mature writer, profoundly inquisitive and sceptical about motives, a master of precise and subtle language, use even this impoverished theme to tell us something worth hearing about ourselves? I don't know. Possibly.

Some subjects may be intrinsically boring. I am always being reminded that in this new age I am an involuntarily impious spectator. Not long ago, in one of the Sunday newspapers I read in the hope, always mortified, that one of the lowing herd will break away from it, I found: 'The convention that described the cut of a man's beard but never the hairs on his razor, the proposal in the conservatory but never the heaving bed-springs, now strikes us as unreal.'

Can I be the only survivor of a generation, rebellious, irreverent towards all sacred monsters, which did not take itself with this comical seriousness? Those bed-springs heaving through the novels of the last two or three decades lack every dimension of meaning except the most commonplace, add as little to our knowledge of George as the hairs on his razor. I can only see ill-bred silliness in the new habit a few talented women novelists have fallen into of describing in clinical detail how they behave in bed, menstruate, or, like the dim young woman in Miss McCarthy's novel, fit a pessary. It is not difficult to describe these things, far less difficult than to expose the hypocrisy and reticences our minds and feelings practise continually, infinitely less difficult than to find adequate words for the emotions involved, their strength, ambivalence, effects. I can't make up my mind whether these writers can possibly have become intellectually convinced that an account of the method a woman uses to avoid pregnancy will give us a clearer sense of her and her life, a new dimension of its sensual reality. What I am quite certain of is that had Tolstoy shown me Anna Karenina fitting a pessary instead of showing me the slow corrosion of her life by her passion for Vronsky I should have yawned and shut the book.

Novels of this school of neo-naturalism bear the relation to literature that a competent snapshot bears to a portrait by an authentic artist, and remain in the mind little longer than it takes to lay the book aside. We know nothing about the familiar bodily habits of Ulysses or Hamlet or Mr Pickwick – we are reduced to supposing them much like our own – but each lives in us more enduringly than our next-door neighbour. We remember Anna Karenina vividly, steadfastly, long after we have forgotten the name and cannot see the gestures of the young woman in *The Group* who suffered *coitus interruptus* with a layabout in New York (or was it Chicago? No matter). The one is a creation in depth, living the mysterious life of a complex literary character, the other thinner than the paper she is printed on. The one was imagined fully, by a powerful mind (not occupied in admiring its own boldness), the other put together like a jig-saw, with patient ingenuity.

I am bored by accounts of the involuntary aspects of a woman's bodily functions, so far from infinite in their variety, in exactly the same way, for the same reasons, as I am bored by laboured descriptions of normal or eccentric sexual acts. And as I am bored by certain sorts of modern art. I am bored by M. Duchamp's notorious urinal, preserved in eight replicas after the lamented disappearance of the original, and exhibited in art galleries, including the Tate Gallery. When I was younger I might have been shaken by learning that certain art critics and philosophers have solemnly decided that it and the other ready-made objects exhibited since, the hat-rack, the shovel, the tin of beans and the rest, became 'aesthetic objects' when the artist picked them out from all the other identical hat-racks and urinals and canned beans in the shop, as if by this act he conferred on them a value they lacked when they left the factory. Now I am mildly surprised when a hypothetically serious critic asks me to accept as valid a definition which rests on nothing but his intuitive certainty that it must be 'true' or, as he might argue, self-evident. To whom? All his oracular statement does is to make empty nonsense of the words *art* and *artist*. If every object a man named or naming himself as an artist picks up and places on show, with or without his signature and thumb mark, is art then nothing is art. Perhaps we should do better not to try to define art at all. Or leave definition to the neo-Aristotelians. Perhaps we could retreat to the less slippery ground of a negative proposition. Decide, perhaps, that an object which can be mechanically reproduced in mass is not art. This would cut out the urinals and the chair with a pipe and a packet of tobacco on it manufactured in chromium-plated steel and labelled 'Van Gogh's Chair'. It leaves in the relentlessly boring stone ovoids and effigies, the crushing silliness of action painting, the whimsical silliness of Picasso's handlebar ram (or is it a goat? Again, no matter).

Applied to literature, it leaves in Molly Bloom (*catin sublime*), Mr Updike's strenuously revolving couples, and the pseudo-bucolic Mellors, and cuts out the bulk of Mr Girodias's *Olympia Reader* and Mr Mailer's masturbating housemaid.

I think I have come on the deepest reason why serious pornography bores me. Any writer, any artist, who presents me with an object, whether it is a hat-rack or an anatomical or other physical detail, which has not been worked over and penetrated by his imagination, is cheating, offering as of authentic human worth what is stereotyped. It doesn't amuse me to be cheated: I regret the waste of time I might have given to *la chasse au bonheur*.

That the language of pornography should be impoverished is inevitable. Literature is not an incitement to action, it is a verbal structure designed to capture and press into words as many subtly evasive feelings and ideas as possible. No distinctively human emotion is simple, and to give an account of a sexual passion involves finding words to raise to the surface a tangled mass of half-inarticulate, turbulent, equivocal motives and sensations. Too naïve and indiscriminating a stress on a single act or gesture brings a clumsy fist down on the finally insoluble contradictions in any human being, even the simplest. Not only is it possible to make a faithful and moving analysis of the sexual experience in all its variety and ambiguity without modish violence, without frothing over like a mustard-pot with the conventional four-letter words, but, freed from these noisy distractions, the naked truth of the experiences blazes clearer, whether in ecstasy, tragedy, or comedy of the earthiest simplest kind.

Charlus remains one of the most impressive erotic figures in literature precisely because he has not been reduced to a stock figure, we are not shown him going through the unvarying motions of the homosexual act. The exquisite comedy of Charlus and Jupien in the courtyard of the Guermantes house, the tragic farce of Charlus in Jupien's brothel – I shudder when I think of the dreary exercise in the ludicrous or the sickening these scenes would have become in the hands of a contemporary pornographer.

In the end, perhaps there are no unusable subjects, there are only good, bad, and mediocre writers. A mass-produced urinal is an unpromising subject for an artist, except in the field of publicity, though possibly a good sculptor, more likely a good painter, using his own tools and a modicum of genius, could make something of it. And that a talented or a great writer can set a character on his stool and elicit from him in that situation what is humanly gay or interesting, witness Rabelais, Saint-Simon, Joyce.

The rest is a bore, *la blague sérieuse*, or publicity.

7. Digression on the Critics

If literary criticism were still, as at various times in the past, a matter of law and precedent (Longinus on the Sublime, neo-Aristotelianism, successive waves of neo-classicism) all would be delightfully smooth and barren. The divine energies and ills that attend on fecundity entered when critics and literary historians began exercising freely their individual tastes. Not, of course, that they became arbitrary and capricious: they stretched their curiosity as far as it would go, climbed metaphysical heights for the sake of the view, paid strict attention to the work they were examining, 'a thing,' said Landor, 'greatly more useful in criticism than is generally thought,' and took pains to draw on as wide a field of comparison as their cultural means allowed.

Well, some did – and do. The others may be a trifle less catholic.

A toiling reviewer of fiction may be guided, modestly or sub-consciously, by the thought: I like this writer because his attitudes and fantasies are the same as my own. Or: I enjoy novels which describe the countryside, foreign parts, adultery, revolution, incest, financial roguery, politics, love. Or: I dislike X., I don't know why, he hasn't harmed me and never will, but he raises my hackles and I have neither the patience nor the humility to overcome my distaste. Or: I detest French literature and writers who seem to admire it. Or: The only novels worth reading or writing are Gidean or Proustian or Joycean or in one way or another experimental. Or: If I don't admire

Y.'s genital variations I shall be looked on as a moth-eaten old ruin.

(This last is the only sensible reason I can give myself to explain the reverent attitude of reviewers – of those reviewers who set the tone in this country – to contemporary pornography. A fear of missing the wind, of being thought timid or intellectually dowdy, a distaste for bourgeois society and its values and prudent pieties? It is of the least importance. What I find wholly inexplicable is their total lack of curiosity about the submerged motives of a novelist who enjoys describing sadistic acts. They must be surprisingly gullible.)

The help modern fiction receives from its reviewers is almost negligible. In part, this may be because most contemporary fiction disappears when a serious critic begins to examine it. We are not without cultivated, intelligent, conscientious reviewers, but so much of the fiction offered them has no very clear connection with literature. A fictional version of gossip about the *mores* of Chelsea or Wakefield, however competently reported, needs the sort of reviewing – an uncritical summary, friendly or damning – it gets. But some part of the blame for the pitiable state of reviewing in this country is chargeable to editors. For one person who will read yet another post-mortem on the body politic a thousand will read a novel, but the amount of space allotted in the columns of journals to reviewing fiction is marginal. And, too, most of these journals now employ casual labour, young men and women in an early stage of their progress through the literary establishment. An intelligent man or woman willing to make a career of reviewing fiction is hard to come by, today especially, when the novel is reputed to be dying. And the temporaries do the work cheaply. Moreover, continuity may be got at the expense of intellectual arthritis; a reviewer who has been at his grisly task for half a lifetime may stiffen into prejudices of every sort, and become too anchylosed to do better than turn his back to a new wave when it rushes down on him.

'We need,' a friend said to me, 'a new Arnold Bennett to review novels.'

'You are wrong,' I told him. 'Lively and acute, he was the literary equivalent of a racing correspondent, useless except to the writer he tipped for that week.'

Reviewing is classed, even by reviewers, in a lower category than criticism. Instinctively, I dislike this outlook, but I should be making a fool of myself if I pretended not to notice the ghastly growth of a reviewers' jargon. I began to make a herbarium, but it was a depressing occupation and I gave it up when I had collected a mere five specimens, all from reputable journals.

From a review of Norman Mailer: 'His problem in the open situation has been to objectify his necessary subjectivity, to pattern the pyrotechnics of his empathising ego.'

'This novel is not as contemporary as – , which I liked immensely, but her exploration of a child's suicide embellishes a somewhat fey area.'

'He writes self-propulsively and aromatically.'

'There is no time to be lost in getting everyone thrown into the great centrifuge of love; because there are to hand squads of significant detail, of easy, surprising symbol-concealing dialogue.'

'– is a considerable creation, a pulse in the eternal groin, a pathetically aborted bog-Prometheus even.'

All in all, it is small wonder that the serious literary critic prefers to put his views on the novel in the more respectable form of a book: a study in depth of a particular writer, or a volume of essays on a few chosen writers (alas, too often the same half-dozen) which allows him to make meditative judgements, to dissect the author or his characters, in brief to show his own paces as an experienced, sensitive, well-educated man.

A vast body of admirable critical work on the novel and novelists flourishes and gives pleasure to experienced, sensitive, well-educated readers. The field is broad, and takes in all the sociological and economic bases of the novel. The works of dead writers are stretched out on the psychoanalyst's couch, or examined through existentialist or marxist lenses. The novel is examined as a super-structure of social pressures, as a form of communication which is partly involuntary, to be exposed by the analyst, as a significant linguistic structure, as almost anything except the spontaneous creative impulse of the writer. It is an occupation for critics who never laugh.

The critic's hankering to be law-giver rather than servant of literature is irrepressible. Throw it out of polite society and it returns with the philosophers and politicians. The heyday of the law-givers lasted so long – from mediaeval schoolmen misreading their Aristotle to the seventeenth and eighteenth century formers of taste. When they were at last, not so much defeated as by-passed, the professional critic became the godfather, appraiser, impartial historian of literature, splendidly incarnated in dear learned epicurean George Saintsbury, and today in René Wellek and the Hegelian subtleties of Eric Auerbach's *Mimesis*.

But the law-givers, like the hosts of Midian, encompass the holy ground. When a writer of the nouveau roman takes to criticism it is more often an explanation, addressed to himself, of his own practice, valuable workshop talk but carrying clear admonitory overtones – *This* is what an intelligent novelist ought to be doing. In the same way the critic trained in a Marxist, a Freudian, a Sartrean school exercises his mild form of terrorism. He does not attempt an impartial judgement of the book under his eye, does not even write literature about literature, which can be very agreeable, so much as found another Order for the instruction of the novice in an intellectual or political or aesthetic creed, to be accepted before the work is even conceived.

None of these creeds is especially abstruse. A newer, even more oracular school, that of the Structuralists, overshadows them, excessively abstruse, a sophisticated mental exercise, and, in the hands of Ronald Barthes and Philippe Sollers, himself a novelist in his hours, something very close to what Valéry said literary history is, a 'vaste fumisterie'. I don't feel entitled to be so impolite. I would rather point to the dangers of retreating into a Platonic realm of forms and essences where the practice of criticism is neglected for the pleasures of constructing scholastically intricate general theories addressed to the circle of initiates.

Need I say that the brilliant speculations of Claude Lévi-Strauss stand in only a godfatherly relation to the new school? Less than godfatherly. Given his impact on two post-war generations, given, too, the modish impulse to classify criticism as a science, almost a branch of cybernetics, they were certain sooner or later to be applied to literature, though not by the master. Structural criticism is an aggressive and esoteric discipline, a rejection of all our preconceptions, intellectual or emotional, of the way a text must be read. Its gnomic eloquence throws a political shadow. Ingeniously – or with superb ingenuousness – it reaches out to involve a rejection of the capitalist way of life (but not with the innocent simplicity of the neo-Marxist ranker). It withers at the root all that green growth of writing-about writing, erecting in its place a theory of linguistics to delight both an Einstein and a Marat of literary criticism. Unlike the gentle Einstein, and like Marat, who believed theologically in the divine right of justice and logic, it demands heads.

I find it hard to decide whether it has any practical value as criticism. Has it an organic relation, however remote, to the human springs of drama and the novel? Or is it a separate literary genre, to be cultivated for its own sake? Well, I think so. There are verbal echoes in it of the fantastic body of writing and speculation poured out by mediaeval alchemists, no less curiously learned, and no more hermetic. I cannot be rid of my sense that the novel is not able to survive a critical operation of the sort carried out by these metaphysical surgeons, dedicated to the study of a text considered as an object closed on itself. What they construct verbally has less significance, less viability, than the secondary structures built up by a writer totally vowed to the concrete, the particular, to *a* human being, his lies, desires, buried motives. We should not be required to read a novel as a musician can learn to read serial music. It is at our peril that we forget that the novel's literary structure is not another less complex version of the structure of a poem. Both exist in and through language, but the language of fiction exists most significantly as a vehicle for an emotional, a moral, a philosophical content. *What* is being exposed is finally more important than *how*. The critic of a poem is surely right to concentrate the finest edge of his attention on its language, to respect the totality of the text, to remember that in another order the words do not convey the same meaning. He may pour out anything that occurs to him as he reads, the feelings, the ideas, it rouses in him, analyse its theme, its versification, but not forget that in doing so he is enriching himself, not the poem. Saddening as it may be to our novelist's vanity to admit that at its most rigorous our language is too diffuse to suffer mortally when our novels are dismantled by the busy investigators of our intentions, the critic of fiction can take much greater liberties.

None of this means that, for the novelist himself, his work is not an indivisible whole, or that to analyse form and content as separable entities is other than a critic's exercise, the composition, learned, intelligent, interesting, what you will, of a species of sub-fiction. The novelist's ruling impulse is to project a manageable world, within which human beings act: form and content rise together in his mind, but the very nature of his impulse to write forces him to devote the greater part of his talents, his spiritual energies, to the content. When the critic separates them for his purposes, stretching the etherised patient on the table, he does not usually kill or maim, though he may not learn a great deal about his subject's living being.

To return briefly to the structuralist. I see no harm, and some good, in a savagely new broom which frightens spiders. But it will be sad if it leads to the use of a new aesthetic jargon by critics hoping to give their efforts a pseudo-scientific look. A structuralist critic is not made by calling everything a language, and talking about the signifier and the signified, and I look forward with alarm to the first work devoted to postulating the linguistic and anthropological structures of the work of – why not? – Ian Fleming, and the reverence, the *bêtise distinguée*, with which it will be received.

That we have spent millions of words discussing Proust's portrait of Parisian society, Joyce's reconstruction of Bloomsday, Tolstoy's theory of history, and the rest of it and the rest of it, testifies to our determination to worry the bones of the novel, and provides pleasant instructive reading for a public avid of instruction. The body of genuinely critical work – stretching from the all but hermetic utterance of Philippe Sollers in France, George Steiner's erudition and the critical authority of F. R. Leavis, to a few admirable monuments of literary history and more or less acute studies of the contemporary scene – is (1) an essential part of the timeless body of culture, (2) enjoyable, and (3) of minimal help to the living novelist struggling to prolong or revive the energies of a perhaps dying genre.

Novelists are too much at the short mercies of reviewers, afflicted at their hands by what George Saintsbury called 'literary currishness and cubbishness (an ignoble but hardy and vivacious pair of brethren)', and by what another and greater man, writing in 1815, called 'boy-graduates in all the technicals, and in all the dirty passions and impudence of anonymous criticism.' (*Biographia Literaria.*)

8.   But thou, that didst appear so fair

But thou, that didst appear so fair
To fond imagination,
Dost rival in the light of day
Her delicate creation.

Wordsworth

That the Hamlet, the Dr Zhivago, the Forsythes of the cinema and the television screen are not the personages who issued from their authors' hands does not need saying. They are their naïve doubles, contrived by an experienced director, using every resource of a powerful industry, from its advanced technical equipment to its flesh and blood actors. The likeness between his contrivance and the original may not be much more than skin-deep. So far as the living novelist is concerned, the sum of money he is paid to abandon his begotten to strangers is normally large enough to stifle any qualms he might feel. Or is he delighted by these handsome changelings? Would it, if he were alive, please John Galsworthy to see audiences weep over the death of Soames as once a million readers wept for Little Nell?

This, the handing out of magnificent prizes to a few writers, is one side of an ambiguous relation between novelist and film. Looked at from another, the film wears the mask of a powerful rival, to be respected and feared, drawing away a potential audience, even a highbrow audience, which might have been spending its time reading, and will – or may – do that only if the spectacle it has been watching started life as a printed book.

'If Balzac were alive today, he would be writing for the screen.'

Perhaps. Certainly he would not need the author of *The Gutenberg Galaxy* to point out to him that a visual language was beginning to challenge the dominance of the written word, and that he was being offered a superb non-verbal way of presenting the human comedy.

The essential concern of the film as shaped by Resnais, Truffaut, Fellini – add what names, French, English, Polish, Italian, Swedish, Czech, Japanese, Spanish, you please – is with a field that used to be the closed estate of the novel. Like the novel, it is concerned to reveal the more or less hidden motives of individuals. Like the novel, it is a narrative form, in the epic or dramatic mode, filtered in the one instance through the mind and senses of the writer, in the other through the shifting camera-eye directed by a human eye and mind. Like the novel, it relates an action, simple or complicated. Like the novel, it deals with ideas as precipitated or crystallised emotions. Like the novel, it implies a criticism of human and social behaviour.

Does it do these things as well as the novelist? Better?

The serious novel is deeply and irrevocably concerned with the reality a man hides – even, unless he is that rare creature, a conscious hypocrite, from himself – under an ostensible concern with ideas, with other people, with class, with social success, or, more subtly, with a scorn of success. This is equally true of novelists as unlike as Tolstoy, Proust, Sarraute, using each his chosen way of approaching reality, as an epic narrator, as an intrepid analyst, as a species of naturalist dredging a pond for animalculae. The impulse is at bottom always the same: to explore the reality of man's life in time to the farthest possible limit, and then to word it. The picture of life a great or a notably intelligent novelist gives involves more than imaginative sympathy and the power to reflect with energy and scepticism on the very bases of human action: the degree of his success rests on his other power to embody them, using his chosen medium. If he had any interest in comparing himself with his film rival, he might say: You make your statement about the realities of human life through a vivid but fleeting vision of them, I subject my readers to a prolonged immersion. Which of us is likely to make the deeper, the more lasting impression?

The impulse of the dedicated novelist, the same in kind in a Tolstoy and a D. H. Lawrence, to sink himself nakedly in the human situation, is essentially religious. And essentially imprudent, reckless of himself, his moral and mental comfort, his very life: Stendhal's passionate devotion of himself *à ne pas se méprendre sur les motifs des actions des hommes, et à ne pas nous tromper dans nos raisonnements* is as much the impulse of a lay saint, a Quixote of the imagination, as Proust's self-dedication to his one great work.

In what way, if in any meaningful way, does this concern of the novel with imaginative truth differ from that of the serious film?

Without ceasing to make certain demands on the ear, the film addresses itself with instantaneous force to the eye, using visual images to convey subtleties of mood and motive which the novelist sends infinitely more slowly through the inner ear of an attentive reader. Handled by a master, the visual image is at once highly evocative and beautifully economical: action and dialogue, received in the same instant, are stripped to the bone, and the conflict between the characters seen with naked clarity. The film can convey the subterraneously directed confusion of a dream through hallucinatory images where a novelist of any school must proceed by the slow process of a verbal language. It can evoke the sense of the past with the same swiftness and economy; a gesture, a fleeting vision, can convey what Balzac needed several hundred words to recall.

The film, moreover, can weave a multiplicity of actions into one fraction of space-time, thus doing easily and smoothly what Sartre tried and awkwardly failed to do in *Sursis*.

It is impossible to read a serious novel without stretching the mind, but a great film, which to be fully understood or 'read' demands strict attention or more than one visit, can *also* be watched, with the minimum of intellectual effort, as a spectacle. There are thus no limits to the size of its potential audience.

These intrinsic virtues of the film, and our new social habits – consider how much that you once got only from books you now get from television: we are becoming a vast tribe of gapers – make it not inconceivable, not obviously absurd, to think that verbal narrative may become a minor or neglected art, and the novelist a nearly extinct species. The great classics will continue to be read in the same spirit as atheists visit Chartres and St Paul's, or as trippers from Manchester and Chicago stare at the ruins of the Parthenon in sunlight, but the living current of art will pass from the novelist to the film-makers as centuries ago it passed from the wandering story-tellers, from the makers of the Iliad and the sagas, to the writer of the printed book.

It is difficult and repugnant to believe that this is possible.

Difficult to think that the novelist's great themes, the nature of man, his memories of the past of his race and his fore-knowledge of its future, his primitive and enduring relation-ships, sex, parenthood, murder, birth, death, and all the distortions in our thought about these forced by changes in the social structure, can ever be handled by the film with the intellectual and nervous intensity and intuitive penetration of a Proust or a Tolstoy.

But these qualities, of intensity and sustained unsentimental penetration, are precisely those lacking in the yearly offerings of our liveliest novelists, in the boisterous verbiage of one, in another's spirited dance among daylight phantoms, in a score of inventive (competent, brilliant, racy, acute, sensitive, amusing, exuberant, startling) anecdotal stories. It would be quite unjust to say that a sense of life is missing in the contemporary novel. And impossible not to find it thin. Clever fingers pick at the knots in the pattern, but the writer's whole self is not involved. Impatient – an impatience I understand only too well – to market his interesting discoveries about people and life, and be paid and praised for them, he passes the tips of his fingers over the surface, and makes his lively report and takes his wage. His involvement in experience is only ankle-deep.

Very few of the works of our so many 'finest living novelists' have qualities that cannot be displayed as competently and spiritedly in the form of a film without loss of depths that were not there to begin with. The lifetime of these very works is sometimes prolonged artificially by translation to the screen, and enjoyed by an audience less and less inclined to prefer the written version. When I remember that the Danes reduced the market for pornographic fiction by ceasing to ban it, I realise that it would shrink further, probably vanish altogether, if the sexual act and its perversions were made free of the screen. Or will do when they are.

What it comes to is that the great film-makers do as well, with fewer demands on the time and patience of an audience, what the ordinarily intelligent novelist does. Sometimes they do it better, persuading us, at least for a short time, for the time between entering and leaving our seats, of the total reality of characters translated from a mediocre novel. Are we to believe that greater or more original novels will be as easily assimilated or surpassed?

I don't believe it. I don't believe that the film will oust them even from places where itself might seem unbeatable, as in its treatment of time. It can play superbly with time, bringing off instantly visual miracles the novelist can only work very slowly. But slowness has certain very great advantages over shock tactics, allowing the sense of time as a dissolving force to penetrate every fibre of the mind, a lasting stain. Attempts to imitate verbally the synchronism of the film – Sartre's dislocated sentences, William Burroughs' cut-ups – fail and deserve to fail: only a clown uses the bow of a fiddle to stir his soup. What makes the famous last scene of *A la recherche du temps perdu* unforgettable is not the spectacle of men and women changed, eroded, by age and their lives – a spectacle the film would have no trouble in presenting – but the vast stretch of time we have crossed to reach it and the felt presence behind the words of Proust's profound knowledge of his personages, itself earned by unsparing and sustained meditation on what he could discover in a ruthless vivisection of them and himself. So it is with the last poignant appearance in *War and Peace* of Natasha, Pierre, Nicholas, Maria, either disillusioned, hardened, resigned, aware only in brief flashes of an ardent past, that past which remains the inalienable possession of the reader. The creator of *War and Peace* is absent from the scene, a *deus absconditus*, but the same overmastering force of time informs both scenes, accepted silently by one writer, overtly mediated by the other. The supple shifts of time in novelists as opposed in their methods as Sterne, Conrad, Joyce, Robbe-Grillet, make their effect not only through the writers' mastery of language but because we are made to take our time to absorb the sensation of time, to feel it as a medium in which we live simultaneously and successively on more than one level.

The man we watch moving, gesticulating, acting, in the film, enabled to watch even his dreams, makes his powerful mark on us quickly. Do we retain the impress as long as we retain the memory of a man the novelist reveals slowly, gradually stripping away appearances, illusions, lies? The quality of the attention and the quality of the response we give the two revelations are quite different.

It is beyond denial that in the cinema great acting and imaginative direction will give us an impressive and moving Anna Karenina: what we shall not receive is the sense we have in reading the novel that we are living with a human being through every phase of a complex interplay of sensual passion and spiritual agony and ecstasy, so various in its turns and twists that we attend to it as to a great symphony. Nor, in front of the screen, shall we have time to notice the extreme subtlety with which her creator compares and contrasts the two greatest sexual themes in literature, that of love as death and love as the fathomless spring feeding a marriage of minds and bodies. Nor time to realise how deeply our understanding of the characters depends on his passionate interest in them as fully moral beings.

Dare I turn this round and say that the woman in any one of Fellini's greatest films would live longer in our minds if she had been conceived in words by a great writer?

The mysterious existence of the characters of fiction is three-stranded. There is the image moving in the writer's mind, engendered from memories of living persons, from things read, or overheard in the street, a newspaper item, a word forced from a woman in fear or delight, the profile of a passing stranger, the whole animated and fused by the writer's total experience, his relations with others, his knowledge of his own most secret motives. There is this multi-celled creature's existence in the words on the page. And there is the image the reader evolves, slowly, only from these words and from the echoes they start up in his mind and send ringing back and back in an infinite regression.

Un roman est comme un archet, la caisse du violon qui rend les sons c'est l'âme du lecteur. (Vie de Henry Brulard.) We pay for the vividness with which a Julien Sorel of the screen assaults our attention by the loss of the complicity between novelist and reader, of the subtle sympathy it engenders, making possible a total response, sensuous and intellectual, to the complex being of the character born and carried to term in the novelist's mind and nerves. Note, too, that in the final reckoning it is not Stendhal's analysis of a particular young man that makes Julien Sorel memorable, richly present with us for our lifetime, like the memory of a living man we loved or hated, it is the concrete vision Stendhal had of him, the completeness with which he saw, heard, and felt him, his relations to the other characters in the novel, and his position in a shifting web of physical and moral activity. The vividness of the film is weaker than the complex vision of the novelist transmitted to us with a fullness and at a depth the screen cannot match.

The languages of film and novel are different in kind. They complement, do not supplant each other. No form of art repeats or imitates successfully all that can be said by another; the writer conveys his experience of life along a channel of communication closed to painter, mathematician, musician, film-maker. The human brain cannot handle, or understand fully, all possible languages, written, plastic, auditive: barriers exist even inside a language, few musically-trained listeners are able to hear both Mozart and Stockhausen.

For the creator of a film, words are largely or wholly subordinate to the image as carriers of the film's total meaning. Certain aspects of life, transposable *directly* into images – signs of progressive mental breakdown, of the profound dislocation of modern society – cannot be instantly transposed into words. The solemn efforts of a few writers to dodge the discipline exacted of them by the nature of language – like that poor young fellow who had holes punched in the pages of his novel 'to give the reader a glimpse of future events' – are unsuccessful on any level, even on the level of the writer's childish trick. The separate words of any given language draw the greater part of their charge of meaning from their context in an intelligible expected order: it is only at the supreme moments of a life (or a death) that a single word torn from the web carries all the meaning of which body and soul are capable – and then only when all that has been said beforehand is sharply present in the mind, as all is still echoing in the ears of the listeners outside Agamemnon's palace when a single cry inside reaches them. The novelist's report on a human life and its possibilities, and his own immensely full and profound involvement in it, demand a language capable of a multiplicity of meanings, of conveying equivocal or discordant trains of thought, at a pace the reader's eye and ear can absorb completely, and – the point of supreme importance – of giving indefinitely renewable pleasure.

So? So only the great novelists are certain of surviving the threat now making itself felt, only they can be certain of defeating a young insolent rival with all the advantages of youth, insolence, and the social habits of the new age on his side? What is dying, undermined by technological progress, enervated by its writers' misuse of language, their obsession with social trivia and the sub-erotic, is the merely good novel?

All things considered, will it matter a great deal if the resources of talent and energy now poured into writing novels with an average lifetime of a few months are diverted to the film? Who knows how this will evolve, what technical triumphs are just below the horizon – a multiple screen, cinema in the round, a score of television channels run off by a single laser beam – to be seized on by writers born to speak the newer language?

I am not willing to take a lighthearted view of the possible defeat of the good minor novelist by television and the cinema. The most spectacular, most intelligent of films would not wholly fill the gap that would be left by the defeat of an

Elizabeth Bowen, a Sybille Bedford, elbowed out by a medium which could not use so delicate a comic spirit, so intelligent a heart. Very rare, the intelligence of the heart. The intelligence of the whimsical brain is less rare, less attaching, sometimes tedious.

Only a literary Calvinist would see nothing to lament in the disappearance of the thoughtful and perceptive novels written by a score of living novelists, or in the killing off by cold of the formal experimenters, the Robbe-Grillets. At the least, they are a valid and charming form of entertainment, a humane pastime; at best, a quickening and widening of our sympathies. They have short lives, but they are agreeable and of good report, as useful to society as a woman remembered after her death by people who pass her house as, 'That charming, clever Mrs Taylor. So friendly, warm-hearted, amusing, witty.' She leaves a gap, they say. Then her house is taken over by a friendly amusing young woman with an architect husband and well-brought-up children, or by two pleasant young men with a talent for interior decoration. Mrs Taylor's ghost fades from the street – which was none the less the better for her life.

In a world on the way to becoming one vast encampment, hemmed in by the compulsion of collectivity, by the incessant bombardment from screen and wireless, we need intelligent fiction as we need every art that, to be enjoyed, demands a measure of privacy. We are in danger of becoming – in another, more insidious sense than that implied by the cult word: alienation – exiles in our world, dwarfed by the great machines and the great buildings in which we do not worship. I believe coolly that the spread of automation into one field of human activity after another desperately needs a human counter-balance. Without it the cancer of dehumanisation and boredom showing itself more and more acutely in our society will spread and spread. 'Where,' asks T. S. Eliot, 'is the wisdom we lost in knowledge? Where is the knowledge we lost in information?' We need the slower and more lasting stimulus of solitary reading as a relief from the pressure on eye, ear and nerves of the torrent of information and entertainment pouring from ever-open electronic jaws. It could end by stupefying us.

9.   Either/Or?

I do not share the pious fears of many better-found critics that the novel is becoming a museum relic. Nor believe that, if it were, the experimental novel – to stretch the term over a score of variations, some intelligent and charming, some naïve, silly, tedious – would save it. Do I believe the other rumour that what is condemned is only the classic or traditional novel?

It is difficult to come by a lucid definition of what its recusants mean by the slippery word: traditional. I can't conceive that all they intend by it is any novel they would not themselves care to write. Or anything so naïve as that no one would now write *Middlemarch* or *The Old Wives Tale*. As reviewers they make our flesh creep by using phrases like two I copied out of one of last Sunday's newspapers: 'One of the few younger writers willing to use a traditional form ...' And: 'In spite of its traditional form, an interesting even dignified novel ...'

To be so astonished that the traditional novel has any qualities that might justify it in being treated as seriously as the latest account of incest or adultery in Pimlico is milliner's or dressmaker's talk: My dear girl, you can't possibly wear a narrow (wide, long, short) skirt, they went out years ago.

There must be a more intelligent motive at work than the impulse to mock the elderly, which is a sound natural impulse, and stores up pleasantly wry memories against the day when the mockers are themselves old dodderers. I could spend time delving for it, but there are questions, more important, I want to ask.

How far is it possible to conceive of a novel which has cut the umbilical cord attaching it to a mental habit that accepted the major task of a serious novelist as twofold, creation (of a world), and criticism (of personal and social values)? How far is every novel, even the most boldly experimental, a closed world, rivalling the actual world? The nineteenth-century novel was just that, a carefully organised world with its own clocks, its own social and political customs, its conforming or rebellious citizens. The mode enclosed writers who might seem to be standing outside, Lautréamont, Apollinaire, Kafka, and, later, the Joyce of *Ulysses* – like Sterne, Joyce was a seminal jet from the centre of the tradition, which threw its seeds and, in the sense that none of his imitators can keep body and soul together, died. None of these abandoned completely the master impulse of the classic novel, a presentation, at as profound a depth as the writer has intellectual and moral energy to reach, of a human being in conflict with society or himself.

Novelists of the 'fifties and 'sixties who seem to escape from the mode (or mould) because they set their novels in a world very unlike the world of writers from George Eliot to Aldous Huxley, are none the less still working within it. To deal boldly, or violently, or gaily, with amoral young women, homosexuals, junkies, rapists, is only to shift the attention (of writer and reader) to an extreme limit of the novels that engrossed readers of Mrs Humphrey Ward and Mrs Annie S. Swan: it is not a recipe for a breakthrough into a new idiom or ethos.

Even novels in which the content is handled with the utmost possible arbitrariness do not escape from the burden of substance, however tenuous, forced on them by language. At the extreme limit there remains the ghost of a world, a nearly invisible thread of narrative in the succession of words and barely intimated acts, an existential duration of endless vacuity.

Even Beckett's anonymous victim, face down in mud, draws breath in a spectral universe.

Dare I conclude that it is an obtuse error to draw a sharp distinction between the traditional novel and the novel seen primarily as an art form? The first is a broad turbulent stream, sweeping up all but the last solitude of the naked soul. Which is Beckett and then silence. The second ignores, more or less overtly, the landscape of social reality, and silhouettes the individual on a background as shifting and hallucinated as that in *Dans le labyrinthe*. The width of the gap between them may nevertheless fall some way short of total separation. The differences between old and new may be only a matter of stress and attitude. The central figure of Christine Brooke-Rose's *Between* is a woman with no settled habitation, no roots in place or person, no very assured grasp of her identity, living, by translating others' words into a second language, a life of repetitive gestures in hotel rooms merging one into another in her mind. Form and content – the novel is laid in an aeroplane in flight – are repetitive, seeming (only seeming) incoherent, asynchronic. Can one say of *Anna Karenina* that the form is as closely identified with the content? In what sense? In the sense that Tolstoy's mental habits forced him to conceive the life of his character in the form in which it exists, as consecutive narrative, articulate dialogue, philosophical statement. Is it impossible for a novelist to be as possessed as Tolstoy by his theme and as possessed by the problem of matching form and content as the author of *Between*, a minor artist, but an artist. Difficult, yes, but impossible? Think of Proust, of the long sinuous sentences fitting like a skin the sinuous exploratory movement of the writer's mind through a society and the minds and hearts of its members.

Il faut être absolument moderne (Rimbaud). Is this true of the novel? Is the novel really separable into a new – barely existent – novel and an old one addressed to a philistine public, even of thoughtful intelligent philistines? Is a synthesis, an evolution of the traditional form, inconceivable? Will it be impossible to write a novel in the old mode with a new intention?

Is the classic novel really inaccessible to vital change? Is there really nothing more of value to be revealed through it about human nature, the heart and its motives, the mind and its greedy lying ways?

Should we now give up looking for the 'great' novels, those which are – in a sense below and above anthropology and archaeology – human history? Content ourselves with the clever ephemeral entertainers, highly skilled purveyors of anecdotes and ideas, sensitive miniaturists, amusing intelligent experimenters? Must we continue to think of the novel in terms of decline and decadence, with all the charms of a decadent civilisation, and no possibility of rebirth?

The classic novels were written by great humanists, men with an enormous appetite for experience, at once greedy and discriminating, driven by it to penetrate human nature in all its dimensions. Essentially an erotic penetration, but an eroticism, a sensual and nervous energy, at the service of a critical intelligence. It would occur neither to Proust nor to George Eliot to reflect that their theme is the entry into the world of the human will – not merely, as today you may be led to think, of the human penis – but they knew it. Their novels were born of their knowledge. Hence what in reading them we discover about ourselves, while it may be disturbing and horrifying, is of infinite worth: even as sexual animals we learn from them more than from the resolutely candid modernist who tells us nothing we did not know, but nothing.

They were not interested primarily in expressing *themselves*. They did that, but they did it with their attention elsewhere, on their vital confrontation – you may prefer contention or *contestation* – with reality.

The metamorphosis of the world in the novelist's mind is incomplete, trite, if he starts from the impulse to express himself, to impart his views about society and the behaviour in it of men and women, often with as little moral or intellectual sensibility as if he were reporting on the manners and habits, including, heaven help us, the sexual manners, of eels. His views may be interesting, like those imparted to us by a fellow-guest at a dinner-party. Unless they start in us trains of thought and feeling which touch the quick of our experience, force us to re-think, re-feel it, to ask ourselves questions about the direction and possibilities of our lives, we forget them in the moment of closing the book.

This is not the common opinion. It is improper to be caught out making an ethical response to, let's say, Genet. Improper to ask of a novel: Does this serve life or decay? Improper or not, I am in no doubt that the narrowly aesthetic response to a novel is, humanly speaking, not ample enough. And that the absence of moral tension and authority in the work of so many living novelists we admire for their cleverness, wit, audacity, and the rest, is a reason why it drops out of mind as soon as read. It is very noticeable that the contemporary novels we remember for any length of time, however brief, with any distinctness, are those whose writers feel a degree of seriousness about human nature and conduct. Those to whom standards of right and wrong, gentleness and cruelty, are not a matter of indifference. It is possible to read through half a dozen clever novels without finding out what their begetters' attitude to life is. Or whether they have one, whether for them life is anything more than a succession of activities, earning money, buying amusements, bringing off a sexual coup. If they leave any mark on our lives at all, it is as vague as the memory of a pleasant or unpleasant taste, or of overheard gossip.

What harm do these dispensers of gossip, of stories of successful and unsuccessful marriages, adulteries, intrigues, do? Surely none. No more than a shower of sooty rain. It remains that their novels were only worth the trouble of writing on the assumption that the novelist is not called on to tell us anything worth listening to about the meaning of our lives. Yet, if he can't do that, if he can't answer the question: Is there any sense in my life? – asked, in the absence of God, by the incurably maimed, the hungry, the tortured, the mother of the murdered child – he should, as we say where I come from, think small, think less of himself than he does when he asks us to think well of him. The noisy or laboured obscenity of one novelist, the easy euphoria of another, the pinchbeck symbolism of a third, the vigorous, spectacular, and finally boring works filled with descriptions more painstaking than Zola's, streams of semi-consciousness, phonographic imitations of speech, the exposure of her feelings by a talented young woman, are operating on the same level as the street clown going through his tricks before a queue waiting at night for the theatre doors to open, some at least of its members anxiously uncertain whether they have come on the right night to the right play.

In their secret hearts, very many ordinary men and women find it intolerable that a tree should live longer than they do. Intolerable, senseless, absurd. Our ancestors' belief in a promised immortality was a refuge, a sure defence against an indifferent universe. Religious ritual protected and appeased. The search for substitute rituals led us lately along some very bloody roads, without reassuring us. Those who now search for 'meaning' in drugs, those who resign themselves to the pleasures of a consumers' society, are not reassured. Perhaps there is no reason why a novelist should think himself called on to put back into our lives the meaning they so clearly lack. Perhaps his need for self-expression, notoriety, and the rest of it and the rest of it, justify him in spending his life writing novels which are forgotten even before he is.

And perhaps not.

Society has changed more, and more radically, in the last two decades than in the two previous centuries. What we see of it now rarely smiles at us, or not with benevolence or a reassuring irony. It has not so truly changed as exploded, inside us and outside. Not merely the nuclear explosion, not merely the moment when men exploded out of the earth's orbit into outer space. Music exploded with the serialists, painting exploded, intuitively with Cézanne, consciously with Picasso, poetry with Apollinaire and the surrealists, the whole conception of art with the *Musée imaginaire*. Sexual ethics have exploded, inwardly with our loss of fear, outwardly in a new social freedom. Something like a rupture with the past of human life on earth has occurred. If the novelist cannot come to terms with it, cannot write from its centre, he might as well hang himself.

You will not tell me that any such novelist is now writing.

Every scribbler now talks of 'a fundamental revision of values'. If he means anything, he means that we have rid ourselves of outworn modes and conventions. But this fundamental revision goes how deep? How deep in the novel? (I can't risk looking any higher.) Only as deep as the novelist's freedom to write descriptions of copulation? That is not very far.

I believe with passion that the quality of life in the emerging society will be determined less by politicians and spawners of creeds and doctrines than by the creators, whether scientists or artists. The either/or position taken up by the – what am I to call them? anti-classicists? – is as crushingly boring as an Albert Hall recital of only one sort of poetry. Never was so much false logic employed in a drier cause. Schoenberg does not, cannot, replace Mozart, nor Philippe Sollers Proust. There is every sort of need and room for the experimental novel, it will open up new levels to a future Proust. So, too, will or may the new criticism. But the guillotine is a clumsy way of making room. The infant Robespierres of criticism (or reviewing) who truly believe that the traditional novel should be relegated to the museum to make more room for – well, you know for whom – will, with the purest intentions, end by creating a dust bowl.

Can I construct a brief aesthetic of the novel as it left the hands of the great and some minor artists? It tries to present the novelist's sensual apprehension of exterior and interior reality through language, the apprehension and the language being part of a single operation, not the theme first and the words fitted to it afterwards. The discovery its author makes of himself is indissolubly part of his discovery of the world – as is a child's. When, with a conscious intention, he begins to relate his intimate knowledge of himself to his observation of the external world (including his fellow-creatures) he is not turning from one task to engage in another, he is looking from another angle at the same human, humanised, reality.

What I rejoice to hope – 'having to construct something upon which to rejoice' – is that a novel with this intellectual and sensuous energy and authority will – not explode – evolve inside a violently exploding society. A traditional novel, written from a ruthlessly modern point of view, taking account of the discoverable forces at work, evil or generous and, as we used to say, decent. A novel you might call a *novum organum* or model, allowing us an insight into human nature and the nature of the world impossible to grasp in any other way, and filling in lacunae in the insights offered us by Marx, Freud, Lévi-Strauss. A novel to help us read our world.

The classic novelist's country is immense, stretching from Tolstoy's inexhaustible interest in society and the individual's struggle to live in it with all the energy of his mind and senses without being crushed by its norms, to the heroic subjectivity of Proust, filtering through his sensibility a particular society from its triumphant peak to its decadence, and a group of characters whose passions and motives he penetrated by way of his own.

With something between malice and deathly boredom I have watched the progress, extraordinarily rapid, of certain talented writers, male and female, from their first steps into what seemed freedom – the freedom to name the parts, produce in full view all the once hidden objects of daily use, relate anything and everything a human being does and says during his days and nights – to their present servitude to the automatic gesture, the grunt-words.

Servitude it is. Imagine the moment of truth when, seeing that four more paragraphs will bring him face to face with the necessity of writing yet another description of the sexual act, of seeking for one, just one, so far unused word and detail, a middle aged novelist stabs himself with his paper-knife.

Pray heaven that even before that glorious moment novelists will be born to us with no impulse to show off an uninhibited knowingness or even a sensitive soul. With, instead, an instinctive awareness of what makes for life and growth and what makes for mindlessness and corruption. With enough energy to persuade by their sane and perhaps arrogant attitude to it that even a society blessed with the means of automation and riddled with bureaucrats (how one sympathises with the angry French student during the late troubles who proposed to hang the last bureaucrat with the entrails of the last capitalist: he forgot that entrails are too slippery to make a good rope) can breed individuals responsible for themselves, their own and their children's lives.

Like that of every other mortal creature, the meaning of the serious novelist's existence and his responsibility suffered a profound shock and change on the 6th of August 1945. He was never an apostle, to promise the resurrection of the body. He could and did promise immortality of a sort, not in so many words, but by the passion of his own belief in the future, in his race of English or French, in the race of man. He can no longer do this. He can promise absolutely nothing to a race condemned by its own inventiveness to live under the threat of sudden annihilation or mutilation in its seed.

Perhaps the question I am really asking is: Why, in such times, write at all?

Only to pass the time?

It is demonstrably a fact that most contemporary fiction seems to have been written with that end in view.

Is this – and the pleasure, for the novelist himself, of venting his mind and heart for our entertainment – good enough? The great novelists thought otherwise.

10. A new language?

It almost seems that the Greeks had no emotions they could not exteriorise completely in the language of Homer and the great dramatists. Classical art had no sediment of inexpressed and inexpressible joy or anxiety. Why? Their philosophy was not particularly comfortable, their gods were indifferent and capricious, or jealous, punishing cruelly the mortal rash enough to challenge them. Is it that any sort of gods, any creative mythology which does not paralyse human reason, is better – that is, more sensually and intellectually vivifying – than none? That, as the gods retreated, becoming shamans, bankers, desert Fathers, what you will, the longings, speculations, curiosity, of our minds and hearts became a raging torrent pressing against words and images quite inadequate to contain it? To body it forth, Carlyle would have said.

So we are left with the modern writer and his romantically 'intolerable wrestle with words and meanings' as our interpreter of an inner world for which no sensuous external correlative exists?

Revolt against the bourgeois morals and manners of his day did not involve the eighteenth, or nineteenth-century novelist in the same wrestle. The verbal approach of the Marquis de Sade was as formal as that of Racine or Stendhal, rested on as settled a social base. The authors of the great nineteenth-century novel used with confidence – with or without a conscious attention to form – the still living language handed down to them. Change there has been since, but change of mood, not of mode. The admirable and admired prose of

Camus and Greene, as committed as their predecessors to a use of words to further narrative and impose an attitude to reality, consciously un-artificial, using a camouflage of the tones of the speaking voice – the artifice of avoiding artifice – belongs as firmly as George Eliot's to a cultivated bourgeois society.

It is noticeable, too, that the slatternly or aggressive writing of A. and B. is as involuntarily directed to a bourgeois audience, though to one which, like the writer, has gone farther along the road to the disintegration of language, private and social. But what is disintegrating, rotting away, on the pages under our eyes is still only the language of an outworn or dying convention, with no green tip of new growth.

What is sinking is the social base that supported even the most violent earlier rebels. Today the novelist starts from a quicksand. Rhetoric, the art of persuasion, was the air breathed by the writer of nineteenth-century fiction. It is anachronistic or forbidden to the problematic post-war novelist of the 'fifties and 'sixties, writing for an unsure, restless, sometimes frightened or jeering audience. If, like D. H. Lawrence, he consciously wants to bring off an intimate fusion of language and human reality as he now feels and conceives it, he cannot happily use a rhetorical mode, cannot, that is, persuade readers to enter a well-established world inside which a succession of events substitutes itself for and claims the privileges of history. Cannot, without stultifying himself, pretend that he is standing on firm ground in a world basically orderly – whatever incidental disorders he is narrating – and go through the intellectual motions appropriate to the pretence. The sequential view of man, living, even when spiritually torn, by rationally explicable motives in a rational world was well served by a language common to George Eliot and Conrad. It is always on the point of breaking in the hand of a contemporary novelist – using the term to cover Joyce, Proust, D. H.

Lawrence, Robbe-Grillet, and to exclude many of their living successors: not every writer is contemporary with his age by being born into it – who must struggle to make himself a tool he can use, as it were, existentially. It will cost him not less than his life, but why else was he born?

Most if not all of today's literary nihilists, of the sillier 'experimenters', of the happy and unhappy exploiters of the obscene, are in ludicrous fact kicking up their heels inside a writing mode handed down to them, however roughly they handle it, rebels in wish, and conventional, or, as they might say themselves, bourgeois, hopelessly bourgeois, without knowing it, in their verbal habits. Any clever mountebank can shuffle pages, or write in the street or night-club idiom of the moment, or dwell on the uses of a pessary, without a trace of feeling for the new possibilities of language. Without any confrontation taking place between today's formidable reality and the consciousness of the writer. The confrontation is dodged. In one way or another. The charming formalism of a novel in which violent acts, incest, murder, are presented like a minuet is a cultivated mannerly dodge. The frenetic assault on our ears delivered by another is the dodge of a clever barbarian, making a noisy scene to distract attention from his failure to communicate anything radically new about the uncertainty and insecurity in which we live.

And since uncertainty is the country we shall be living in, so far as one can see, for the rest of our time on the planet, the novelist will eventually have to learn to inhabit it like a self-possessed well-informed native. Feeling no need, as a writer, to demonstrate for or against sexual freedom, communism, scientific mayhem and the infinite rest of it, as consumedly occupied with the theatre of the human passions as Stendhal ('Ecrire autres choses que l'analyse du coeur humaine m'ennuie.') and Proust, and with energy to spare for the effort of using language to reflect intimately a reality in which the only constant is the movement itself of passion. Passion of a great prince or of a baker who is a cuckold.

It is infinitely beyond my powers to suggest to the novelist of the present or future how to find a verbal approach to the new reality. If I knew I would not be writing about it. I would be writing.

As it is, I have only prejudices, ideas, doubts. In a civilisation fractured as is ours by the collapse of traditions, violent change in styles of living, threatened (if that is not too rough a word) by something like a mutation of the species, *can* a writer sink himself so completely in it that his language is the language of a fully aware human being, and not that of a member of a class or a group, even a large group? The one belief – or prejudice – I hold firmly is that insecurity and disorder are not most intimately expressed by disordered language, just as I do not feel that Picasso's *Guernica* offered a very profound or evocative vision of terror. My strong instinct is that a powerful emotional charge is conveyed by a prose of extreme nakedness and dryness better, with more authority, than by any other.

I repeat myself? Very well, I repeat myself.

Be that as it may, I am clear that the task of fitting our deepest, most primitive or most sophisticated impulses into a new context, of exploring and revaluing all our emotional habits, all our values, is only bungled by assaults on the ancient and delicate habit of language we call syntax. If a complete break with its multitudinous roots and fibres were possible, it would be a death, not a rebirth. There is a limit to what can be represented in and by words, what Wittgenstein called *die Grenze der Sprache*. Language is in varying degrees, but unavoidably, representational; all attempts to overleap the bounds thus set to its uses land the bold would-be violater in confusion and non-sense, or in bombast. The impulse to push against these boundaries, to set foot inside the unsayable, is perhaps the deepest impulse of the creator. A great poet can risk it. It can be done in prose by hints, by starting up echoes in the reader's mind, or in what Kierkegaard called 'indirect discourse' – think how close, in *Fear and Trembling*, he comes to saying the unsayable – but not by brutally dismembering it.

For the novelist, it is more important to know what one can say than to startle by inventing a use for words which is, humanly speaking, mis-use and noise. A geological shift in the structure of speech would, if it could be made, break off the writer's relations with reality exactly as a psychotic does when he invents a totally private language.

A prose of extreme dryness and nakedness – well, yes. But at the same time a prose supple enough to turn and twist with the novelist through the labyrinth of his own mind and heart and the appalling confusion outside.

The novelist's duty to language: to struggle against its voluptuous enchantments; to grip this Proteus until it submits. It will never submit. An imperfect tool is all he has in hand to shape his meaning. The poet and his intolerable wrestle, or less exaltedly, the comedian –

> 'And there he plays extravagant matches
>> In fitless finger-stalls
>> On a cloth untrue
>> With a twisted cue
> And elliptical billiard balls.'

Poets – even a novelist or two – have dreamed of a one-to-one correspondence between language and reality. It doesn't and cannot exist. Yet, morally, sensually, ethically, aesthetically, the writer cannot afford the mental relief of admitting to himself that there is an unbridgeable gap between language, written or thought, and reality, exterior or interior. He must sometimes believe as humbly as a Christian believes in the Truth handed down to him that he can carry across the gap *a* truth, *a* reality worth the metaphysical cost of carriage.

*

It is possible that a revolution in literature and the other arts proceeds at first by regression, by turning the back on all traditional forms which can at least seem to block the way forward with their frozen bodies. Painters discard almost everything their great ancestors lived by, and produce primitives, cubism, Picasso and his dwarfish followers; at the next to the lowest level a few Jackson Pollocks, children splashing gloriously in a puddle of colours; at the lowest – make your own choice. Writers discard Balzacian descriptions, the humane pudor of *Middlemarch* or *Wuthering Heights* or *Nostromo*, and the elegancies of syntax and grammar: their Anna Kareninas menstruate, abort, copulate in public: we reach the delighted absorption of the child playing with his private parts. This must surely be the point at which the wheel begins imperceptibly to turn upward. But what is to come of this regressive-progression, what genuine new form, is not yet apparent. Every sort of gallant attempt, nouveaux romans, will precede it.

Since I believe that the raison d'être, or excuse, of fiction is and must be, in the first place, its content – the discovery of himself by Stendhal, of the narrator of *A la recherche du temps perdu* by Proust, and their efforts to create a society, whether a society of two or of a class, a nation, a continent – I believe that the novelist's language must be a medium in common use in his time, which he must struggle to make both precise and evocative. In his hands it remains a tool in a sense which does not apply in music or painting. It will not be current speech; it is speech organised for a purpose not primarily aesthetic. The language of *Dans le labyrinthe* and other nouveaux romans is organised to approximate to the flux of life on a level of sensation. Deeply interesting and engaging so far as it goes, which is much less far than Proust. Or Tolstoy. And would be boring if it were prolonged.

Progress is here a meaningless term. The art of the novel does not progress, any more than painting has progressed since the prehistoric cave artists, or sculpture since Crete. We know as much about the spiritual cost to a man of taking on himself to punish with death a mother, a son, a brother, as did the author of the *Oresteia*, not more. The spiritual history of the novel passes from summit to summit, Stendhal, the great Russians, Balzac, George Eliot – begin where you like, end where you like. They differ from each other not in size, but only in the energy and authority with which they impose their vision of reality on us through their use of language.

11. A new beginning

What went ye out for to see? A novelist able to take the atrocious confusion and dread of today's world into his mind and heart and give it back metamorphosed, transfigured, its hell-dark corners blazing with light, its very terrors standing out as clearly as white columns on a Greek headland? A novelist cool enough to stare back at our instinct for cruelty and death, and affirm its opposite? Able, without breaking down under a crushing burden of insights and emotions, to set his novel down in Auschwitz as steadily as in London or East Coker?

He doesn't exist. But there is always the chance that he will be born, the chance of genius turning up in a new writer, a Mozart of the novel, for whom the truth of life in our time will be naturally, in pain and pleasure, comprehensible and able to be sung. It will not matter whether he discovers that the truth is strictly unbearable, so long as he can say so calmly and triumphantly. Or whether he feels about human beings that they are irredeemably pitiable and often pitiless, provided that he feels an infinite pity for these feeble creatures and an infinite respect for their efforts to live responsibly.

We shall not ask him to give final answers, these will not be in his reach, but only to give himself the trouble to ask the final questions: after all, there is no such thing on earth as absolute reality – whatever meaning we separately attach to the term – all our meanings are relative; every question has to be asked and answered afresh in the light of every generation's peculiar hope and anguish. Nor do we want him to make himself responsible for our happiness. If we cannot pursue that for ourselves, we deserve to be cheated of it and of our freedom by bureaucrats and party leaders. Nor shall we object to his showing arrogance, provided he joins to it the humility of a writer who knows how far he is from plumbing the depths of one simple human being.

For pity's sake let us stop moaning about our alienation, and accept a little calmly our loss of moral and social standards that only someone born before 1914 can shadowily recall. We can no more turn back to George Eliot's or Tolstoy's image of man at the centre of a now inexistent order than we can return to Homer's. The absence of time-honoured standards is what the contemporary novelist has to start from. And has to accept that the evil outside – Hiroshima, the death camps, wars in which children die of hunger or seared by napalm – is a mirror image of what goes on inside himself in solitude, and, with what coolness he can, use intelligence and technical mastery to make sense of it.

One, if not the sharpest, challenge to his imaginative understanding – as sharp as the smiling indifference of Olympus was to the Greek dramatist and the mysteries of time and death to mediaeval poets – is the ironical truth that the labours of the reasoning intellect have armed the darkest irrational fears and greeds of man with power to destroy himself and the planet. We have to accept this, and accept, too, that communism, the most rational of ideologies, the one sworn to compassion for the dispossessed, has issued in cruelties equalled only by the irrational excesses of fascism.

On reflection, I wonder whether this self-betrayal of reason is not rather a question of practising, behind the mask of reason and ideology, very old pleasures that, for our comfort, we prefer to think of as belonging to the devil's part.

No modern novelist has found the imaginative energy to give flesh and blood to ambiguities and a vision of absurdity and anguish as bottomless as hell. Possibly the one who will is being born at this moment. The effort to find *in himself* a firm ground of memory and hope under the confusion and stand on it to write will be inconceivably hard. He will be a fool if he rests any certain hope on the future, and a greater fool to despair, or fail to rejoice in any excuse for happiness, from a clear June morning to the *Nozze di Figaro*.

Fifth-century Greece and Elizabethan England – not calm untorn countries – gave an easy birth to superb comedies. We might remind ourselves that the values of modern civilisation have been in danger for a long time, from the moment the first men spared a thought for anything other than their bodies' needs. There is never a time when civilisation can be called safe, as certainly as there is never a moment when the most civilised of men is safe from the impulse to cheat or murder. Never, before now, has the mind of man been so fatally at the mercy of its worst dreams. Since anger and a desperate looking the other way are both useless against them, laughter can do no harm and may even do a little to civilise the tribe.

Ours is certainly a hell of an age to get on terms with – not for its inhumanity alone but for its strident vulgarity and in-difference to what is only old, simple, fine – but a novelist, great or small, has no more imperative use for his intelligence. The deeper the tensions, conscious or unconscious, in his mind, the better his chance, if he has the insolence and reckless cour-age, of meeting head on the sharpest contradictions and anguish of his day. Whether he makes tragedy, comedy, or farce of them is his business. This is true of writers as dissimilar as Brecht and Malraux (before he became a functionary). And of some lesser writers: what, if not the struggle to hold to-gether two ends always on the point of flying apart in him, gives Graham Greene his degree of intensity?

It was never so difficult as now to create a world which can stand over against the one we live in, insecurely and in danger of destruction. We have not managed to control, and cannot cancel, the new forms of civilisation. (Ironically – but it would not have surprised the old dead woman who warned a child that 'ill weeds grow apace' – the most triumphant culture of our day, now split like sour green wood on one side into a thorough-going commercialism and on the other into a pitiful sick defeat, is the negative one of pop. Negative in the double sense that it rejects the past and has nothing to offer the future.) The responsible novelist cannot, much as he might like to, withdraw into a centrally-heated monastery. But he is no longer a member of a society whose values he shares: with at least half his mind he is thinking and feeling against the currents of the age, and tormented by their complexity. Yet, if he is to survive as a living force, he will either make the frightful effort to hear, under the distracting noises, the deep single note of life itself – or give up and leave the field to the film-makers with their illusion of a one-to-one correspondence between their images and reality.

What it comes down to is simple and awful. The novelist has one sure resource, only one, in a struggle to make himself heard above the loud electronic noises. This is to create in depth, to uncover with more and more subtlety and truth his total experience, to press into his words more meanings than can be broadcast or televised or filmed. To make himself master of a language which will bear the weight of all he knows about the reality that lives through us and we understand so weakly.

This involves something so exacting that few of us care to look it in the face. A writer is not forced – unless a dictator forces him – to be useful; he is not, now, forced even to trouble himself about the social effect of his work – if his conscience does not trouble him, the police will not. But what he will be forced to do – if he is to survive as something more than a spectator and reporter of the modern world, or as a clever amusing startling (anything you like) literary haberdasher with a weather eye on his new powerful competitors – is to write fewer novels. Far fewer. Which will be good for his soul though not, if he hoped to live by writing them, for his belly.

This is something about which I am so certain that I make no apology for saying bluntly: I *know*. As a serious-minded novelist who has made a living by writing far too much, I say that the habit of writing to pay the bills is deplorable, pitiable, foolhardy – choose your own epithet. This was always true. It is true a hundredfold now, when your craftsman writer is in competition with machines that can outbid him in diversity of entertainment on every level *except the highest*. In the future there will be no level left wholly free for him except the one that can be lived on only by a master, he who can answer questions, about love and ambition, mercy and cruelty, birth and death, it will be no use putting to the most carefully programmed computer, or hoping to have answered in the television studio for the flapping ears of a million listeners.

What the embryo novelist should be told, at the first moment he shows signs of an ambition to be other than a competent entertainer or social commentator, is: Earn your living in a way that does not draw on your imagination, your love of words, and write your novel slowly, over a long time, unlimited time, with unlimited patience, enriching it by all you learn as you go. Hand yourself over naked as a babe to your vocation. If, like Proust, you have arranged to be born with a private income, your task will be that much easier, but not less heroic. Lacking a private income, you can look on yourself as a secular saint, prepared to wait ten, twenty, years – while laying bricks or making machine tools or serving as a consul – before producing your *summa mundi*, your dialectic between man and society, or your quintessential report from the depths. If all you want to do is to write about clouds, rainy streets, seagulls, cracked pointed shoes, blown hair, with divine accuracy, why not? It is very difficult. You need not even be a great innovator. If you can only say what you have to say in a new form, however outrageously revolutionary, do so, and if you can use the old forms to carry a new emotional charge, use them. Either way, Apollo be with you. With his blessing, you may find in your study of a rejected lover or a social rebel a nuance or a word that Stendhal missed.

Am I describing a monster? Or talking about a writer the equal in his field of Einstein in his? You don't expect an Einstein to make a statement of his findings every twelve-month. Why expect it of a dedicated novelist?

Nothing I am saying is new, or apt only today. 'With no other privilege than that of sympathy and fair wishes, I would address an affectionate exhortation to the youthful *literati*, grounded in my own experience. It will be short; for the beginning, middle and end converge in one charge: *Never pursue literature as a trade.*' (*Biographia Literaria:* 1817.)

Grace of tone apart, just what I was saying.

*

It is conceivable that human life, in a universe which can get on very well without man, is basically absurd and meaning-less. Perhaps the only meaning it has is put there by Bach and Rembrandt and Blake and their fellows. It is conceivable. In any event, no good reason why a great novelist should not write *as if* he were the creator of meaning, and a great many why he should. Man running loose in a meaningless world is apt to be a dull mischievous often murderous bore.

This, finally, is why I cannot be satisfied with a narrowly aesthetic judgement on all those contemporary novelists – from the urbane raisonneur, Robbe-Grillet, to the unreasoning infantile bagmen of fiction – who, in their work, repudiate the few constants in human nature: its endless attempts to achieve a system of logical thought, its endless turning back to a few basic moral notions, of justice, fraternity, love, to be prized even above courage, which moreover these imply, and without which man would not exist.

Since the birth of consciousness, the spirit of man has been nourished by a remarkably few myths – remarkable that they are so few – kept in remote memory in the artist's imagination. The imagination is conservative at a deep level precisely because it is rooted in these few underground seed-beds of thought and feeling, and goes back and back, like a tide pulled by the moon, to draw its energy from them. Cut off from them – as in a mechanised society it too easily is – it withers into fancy, naïve, romantic, obscene, or chokes on nihilistic despair or anger. Even a weak myth has power of a sort: I learned this when, one evening in January 1968, I went to a revival of Shaw's *Heartbreak House*. It is not a very good play, the characters are two-dimensional, the poetic energy of the first act does not last, but, at the end, when the bombs fell, I was put to it not to weep bitter tears – for our heartbreak as a country, for the young dead of that war, for the withering away of the myth of their England.

Many persons can tell us what to do to avert the material dangers forced on us by our own ingenuity. Only the imaginative artist can keep alive the image of a whole man able to feel life with his intellect and think with his body, and he only when some nerve of his mind reaches down, even sporadically, to the mythical roots of thought.

Les hommes n'ont guère en commun que de dormir quand ils dorment sans rêves – et d'être morts . . . True, true. It would be absurd to expect of the novelist that he can do more than mitigate the final solitude, the final absence – at a level below the level where the roots meet and merge – of communication between man and man. What, with one mythopoeic eye open, he can do is remind us how, at what cost, the individual can

147

escape becoming nothing more than a unit co-existing with the other units of an atomised society.

It is small use speculating about the form the unwritten new novel will take, but why not speculate? Possibly the handiest method of mastering confusion and complexity, of presenting lucidly the greatest weight of experience, may be Proust's of merging the novelist with the memorialist and the infinitely inquisitive observer, Saint-Simon, Montaigne, Jean-Jacques Rousseau. In a sense, this is little more than a shift of stress. The classic novelists did not have to wait for Freud to be born to know everything about the quarrel between the *moi social*, continually adapting itself to life in its world, defending itself by lies, hypocrisy, evasions, ignoring or dismissing or failing even to recognise its own motives, and the *moi profonde*, the self known wholly to no person, not even to itself, pursuing its needs and desires in silence and darkness. They used their know-ledge intuitively, with varying degrees of subtlety and bold-ness, to present characters detached from them. The distinctive habit of the modern novelist is to include himself and his sensibility in his contemplation, merging the perceived object with the perceiving subject. With relentless scepticism, Proust observes himself observing, accompanies himself vigilantly in his pursuit of the secret self of *the other*. His greatness springs from his dedication to the double effort, the chase, mediated through himself, of the *moi profonde*, and the presentation in great detail of the *moi social* and its world. What except the accident that he has not been born yet, stands between us and a novelist able to join the subtle charity for fallible men and women of a Proust to the sensuous density of a Tolstoy, the energy and gaiety of a Stendhal?

All we have to do is to wait for the birth – with a private income or the courage to do without it – of a major writer created to give birth in a novel to the new age. Or re-birth.

'What do you expect this phoenix to do?'

Entertain me. Exhilarate me. Place the novel in the service of life and growth, even when he is probing the infernal depths of our cruelty. See to it that the doubts of ourselves his probing rouses in us are not mean doubts. Encourage every creature to live uncrushed by his inevitable failures and humiliations. Create, and imprint on our minds by every sensuous formal means in his power, beings so densely living that they outlast many merely human lifetimes.

Perhaps what is wanted is a tragic optimism.

One thing I am sure of. Novelists who treat violence and cruelty as something to be exploited for their effect, or to enjoy the pleasure of an evacuation, are carriers of a singularly unpleasant disease. Reading, we receive from the page not only what the novelist wrote there, but his attitude to it, which betrays itself even against his will. I am very conscious that when I reject *The Naked Lunch*, or Genet's over-rich, clotted, didactic, and finally boring monologues – only his first novel was a spontaneous jet of truth from a child's hell – I am rejecting not simply a particular work but the effort to communicate with the mind behind it.

So? So I have a polite right to choose what company I keep.

I see no compelling reason to put obstacles in the way of anyone minded to read a very highly praised novel – one English critic welcomed it as 'the first great novel of masturbation'. I daresay it is the first. To be exact, it is not a pornographic work, in the sense commonly given the term. It is relentlessly and excitedly indecent, but that is something else. I shall avoid its author's company in future only because of an entirely involuntary nervous failing: physically offensive people and acts make me frightfully uncomfortable, like being forced to swallow the skin of rice pudding or handle greasy dishes. A less egotistical reason for avoiding it would rest on George Orwell's saying: 'Human society must be based on common decency' – supposing, as I do, that he meant to stretch the term a little, to cover small private reticences as well as public ones.

It was never more necessary·than at this moment for the writer, novelist or dramatist, to look directly at cruelty and incoherence – if he is mature enough, clearheaded enough, sanely sensuous enough, to do it with intelligence, however harsh, ironical, amused, and without shuddering or wallowing, or becoming hysterical and bawling at the top of his voice. We shall never grasp the human reality of, say, Belsen until it has been fused and shaped in the imagination of an unborn Dostoevsky. The death of Julien Sorel, the end of Mother Courage, are brutal – and vitally exciting because they witness that a few men and women can endure anything. The ungenial obscenities of *The Naked Lunch* and its kind are only clumsy and beyond words depressing.

Heaven knows I am no neo-Aristotelian critic, happy with only one kind of novel, even only one kind of great novel. Dearly as I would like to be seen sitting at the high table with critics and writers in vogue, I should not long be at ease there. I am too profoundly convinced that there is no one right or solely respectable form of fiction, no one technique. No sacrosanct rules. Given the devouring energy, the endless and sceptical curiosity of the great novelists, almost any tool will serve. Certain are better adapted to the work than others, but at times a blunt axe will serve for something – witness Dreiser in his moments. The only bad style is one that tries to produce an effect by non-literary means, from concrete poetry to fold-ins, cut-ups, and what have you.

I don't hope for more than one writer in a generation (or two, or three) to be willing to dedicate himself to writing as few as five novels in his lifetime. While waiting for him to be born, no one can be better pleased than I am with any novel from which I draw a modicum of intellectual, spiritual, aesthetic enrichment and *pleasure*, any novel I can re-read, any that tastes so sharply of itself that the first reading does not sate. All I insist on is a touch of frugality in the overworked themes of mindless violence and sex, gaiety of a two-edged Mozartian sort, and a kind of writing that gives me sensual delight even when it is disturbing me, horribly, by its strangeness, intensity, grief, fury, imaginative boldness.

One novel I want, from a Turgenev of the 'seventies or 'eighties – I cannot be sure of lasting longer – is a new *Fathers and Sons*. It will be a pity if the master film-makers produce it first.

There are moments when I overhear myself thinking that what we need in this country, novelists, playwrights, poets, is a measure of persecution, to bring home to us the value and ambiguity of words. We might pay more attention to grooming them if political pressure, daring us to risk something, forced our energy and wits to run the soft slack flesh off their bones. Take the characters and incidents of any entertaining, exuberant, shocking, witty novel of the season and imagine them passing through the mind of a Polish, Russian, Czech writer; the finished novel might be just as ephemeral and none the less carry a charge of meaning, an underlying urgency, missing from its easy come and go English counterpart.

Or a fifty-year ban on writing fiction? Think of the spontaneity, devotion, energy, love, with which, when it was lifted, writers would plunge into the human tragi-comedy, curious about every aspect of it, from *l'enfant amoureux de cartes et d'estampes* to the solitary old man dying his own death. Only to think about it gives me a few minutes of acute happiness.

Epilogue
(for H.B.)

Do I set too much store by intellectual and moral elegance? I think not. I think, and shall impenitently think until I cease thinking, that slovenly writing – the automatic response to experience, the flabby half-exact phrase – is inexcusable. Not unforgivable, in the sense that the exploiters of sexual abjection are unforgivable, because of the stain of cruelty they spread through the fabric of society, but strictly without excuse. In the end the debasement of language is an infinitely greater fault than clipping the coinage, does more harm.

My situation as a writer is the unenviable one of a survivor. My ears and other senses are a survivor's. Not only because of my age. Not only in the sense that anyone who came to consciousness of himself before 1914 belongs to the last years of an era which includes the Greece of Pericles, Byzantium, the building of the great cathedrals, the French Revolution, Stendhal, Mozart, Baudelaire, the discoveries of Newton, nineteenth-century French painting, and ended in August 1914, brutally. Certainly my birth colours my outlook on life and letters, even against my reason. I had curious evidence of this two years ago. Confronted, when Robert Lowell was rejected for the Oxford Chair of Poetry in favour of Edmund Blunden, by the angry contempt of my most intelligent friend, a young man – 'What excuse,' he demanded, 'is there for choosing an old man rather than a younger and more distinguished poet infinitely closer to the pulses and needs of the age we live in?' – I could only feel that, though he was in a degree right to put the choice down to stiffened joints, he was wholly wrong. The electors, many of them of Blunden's age, had not chosen between two poets, they had voted for the author of *Undertones of War* and, some of them, for a boy who was killed at Ypres or Loos or Gallipoli before he had had time to write his poetry, or, like Wilfred Owen, when he had only begun to write it. He was right in so far as it is true that England, which in the past gave birth to some of the greatest poets in the world, cares little for them – not wholly a bad thing: carelessness is better than the artificial stimulants now being administered to poetry, by the B B C, the Arts Council, self-advertising stunts like the Albert Hall meeting, all likely to do more and subtler harm to any young writer than neglect.

I say nothing about the respective merits of the two poets.

My journey since, without knowing it, I began to be a survivor has been that of a questing middleclass (in every sense) writer and intellectual of pre-war birth, unable to accept that the world she regarded as enduring, even after the bloody harrow of 1914-1918 had passed over it, is in ruins. I cannot help my instinctive hostility to the intellectual and spiritual character of the present, its mindless disbelief in simplicity and simple goodness, its hysteria, its plebeian servitude to fashions (aesthetic, literary). I cannot stop myself seeking in new writers for a meaning – related to lost standards of value – they cannot offer, or offer only clumsily and as it were by inadvertence. I am not oblivious of immediate reality, I don't take windmills for giants, or sheep for enemies – though a biting sheep is a vicious animal, as I have good reason to know – but I cannot live, not *live*, in the tatty world of pop art, scatalogical self-indulgence passing itself off as literature, wilful inelegance in public and private manners.

I should add that my solitude is my own fault. The young of my generation were slow coming to maturity. And I was born with a distaste for coteries, even of the distinguished. It is one of the worst flaws in my character. No wonder I feel so little shame in maintaining that the traditional novel is still infinitely viable, more viable than its short-breathed successor.

I am bored, lethally bored, bored in the marrow of my being, by ninety-nine out of a hundred new novels put before me as worth attention. Without conscious impulse I make demands on them which are not made now. A gap I cannot cross has opened between me and a world in which too often I find myself posing awkwardly as *souffre-douleur* or scarecrow. It used to grieve me. Now I put up with it cheerfully enough, as one learns to put up with a snub nose. The role does not charm me, but there is nothing I can do about it, and nothing sillier than an alien pretending to admire manners, cults, enthusiasms, he cannot share. None the less it is sometimes a little sad to be always out of step, feeling and thinking in one world and existing in another. If I were not the sanest of northerners I might have gone mad.

Hence my instinctive search for another society, and my romantic view of France as the country which – until now – has kept a just relation between the mechanised and natural sides of life, kept the salt and honey of a culture founded on wine and good bread. A personal myth, but a vital one, allowing me to breathe. Hence, too, my long love-affair with Stendhal.

I could justify my admiration of him by talking at length about his peculiar genius, about a habit of mind which takes up the contradictions and hidden motives of human nature with a smiling irony and a gaiety as profoundly real and profoundly sad as Mozart's. About the incomparable pleasure given by novels with the supple energy of young athletes stripped for a race. It would be less disingenuous simply to echo old curmudgeonly Paul Léautaud – *Chez Stendhal, l'homme est si particulier, qu'il n'y a pas de milieu: on l'adore ou on le déteste.* How could I not love a man who, throughout a life never, except for a very few years, easy, declined to lift a finger to cultivate an important man merely because he might be useful and who blamed no one and nothing but his own nature for his lack of worldly success?

He has had little influence on later writers. He is a cult rather than an influence. It is not simply that as a writer he is inimitable: as much can be said of Proust and Joyce, which has not saved us from a seedy mob of proustifying and joycean novelists. It may be that the man caught sight of in his letters and journals, and in superb fragmentary autobiographies, exercises so powerful a fascination that interest in him is channelled into curiosity about his life, every reachable cranny of which has been explored. The fact remains that a novelist can be soaked in his work, as Jean Dutourd is, without his own novels showing a trace of the master's influence. The obvious apparent exception, Jean Giono in his later work, is a proof that no one can be influenced by Stendhal by wanting to be: long stretches of the admirable novels about Angelo, from *Le hussard sur le toit* onwards, read like pastiche.

A writer can be influenced by a predecessor only – except in superficial ways – if he is capable of responding at a great depth to the intimate movement of the older writer's mind, if, as a writer, he shares the same blood type. I suspect that this sort of transfusion is infinitely rarer than is generally allowed. Or that certain men, Stendhal one of them, have a blood type so rare that it cannot be accepted by any but the one person in a million with the same type in his writer's veins: Giuseppe di Lampedusa may well be the only novelist to have been deeply and subtly taught by Stendhal, and his one novel the single work that would not have been what it is but for its author's feeling for Stendhal.

The little I was capable of learning from him I learned badly. But it sharpened my innate distaste for certain forms of writing, for exaggerated eloquence, wilful obscurity, botched slipshod language. It hardened me in my obsessive belief that a writer's first duty is to be clear.

Clarity is an excellent virtue. Like all virtues it can be pursued at ruinous cost. Paid, so far as I am concerned, joyfully.

I am prepared to take enormous trouble to penetrate any writer's obscurities, real or apparent, but only if his obscurity is not mere verbal acrobatics, romantic barbarism, or a sottish failure to make himself clear to a friendly scrupulous reader. Boredom, or spleen, gets the better of me when I suspect that I am not meant to understand, but only to accept the words, in a gush of sensibility. And that my effort to understand him will be taken by the author as evidence of lack of subtlety. Worse, of trying to use an inferior, not to say traditional, method of comprehension.

Style is no less, no more, than the writer's individual attitude to form and content. Its deep roots are mythological and biological, not historical, not social. It is intentional in a sense outside history. This in spite of the fact that a novelist is forced to write inside his society or some particular area of it. I write from the still warm ashes of a society given me by my birth and growth in it, I cannot write in the language of any other. If this begins to lose its idiomatic cogency when I am too old to learn to think and feel in the new idiom I become a survivor, talking my obsolete personally shaped language to deaf ears. The past remains to me, as strong and hard as Yorkshire stone, as green as a sapling. Luckily, to my intense happiness, I may still use my ears and eyes.

About the Author

STORM JAMESON was born and brought up in the small Yorkshire seaport of Whitby, where her family had been settled for six hundred years. She graduated from Leeds University with a First Class Honours degree in English Literature and Language. From Leeds she went to a John Rutson research fellowship at London University, where she obtained her M.A. for a thesis on modern drama in Europe.

From 1923 to 1928 Storm Jameson acted as the London representative for an American publisher. During this time she came into contact with many of the writers and artists in England, and the experiences and friendships gained during this period were a great asset to her when, in 1939, she became president of the London center of the P.E.N. She is now a vice-president of the P.E.N. Club.

In the autumn of 1945 Storm Jameson traveled to Poland at the invitation of the Polish Government, and then to Czechoslovakia, where she was the guest of the Czech Ministry of Foreign Affairs. Her feelings when passing through some of the most devastated areas of Eastern Europe are vividly described in her autobiography. Although Miss Jameson says that she is "a provincial at heart," she has a most perceptive understanding of the relations between the different nationalities and cultures. Some of her best known novels have European settings. Her books have been translated into German, Czech, French, Swedish, Danish, Norwegian, Spanish, Polish and Italian.

She is married to Professor Guy Chapman.